T0303091

THE FUTURE OF WARFARE

Global Economic Trends and the Future of Warfare

The Changing Global Environment and Its Implications for the U.S. Air Force

HOWARD J. SHATZ AND NATHAN CHANDLER

RAND PROJECT AIR FORCE

Prepared for the United States Air Force
Approved for public release; distribution unlimited

For more information on this publication, visit www.rand.org/t/RR2849z4

Library of Congress Cataloging-in-Publication Data is available for this publication.
ISBN: 978-1-9774-0298-1

Published by the RAND Corporation, Santa Monica, Calif.

Cover: metamorworks/Adobe Stock
Spine: combo1982/Getty Images, matejmo/Getty Images, StudioM1/Getty Images

Preface

Where will the next war occur? Who will fight in it? Why will it occur? How will it be fought? Researchers with RAND Project AIR FORCE's Strategy and Doctrine Program attempted to answer these questions about the future of warfare—specifically, those conflicts that will drive a U.S. and U.S. Air Force response—by examining the key geopolitical, economic, environmental, geographic, legal, informational, and military trends that will shape the contours of conflict between now and 2030. This report on global economic trends and the future of warfare is one of a series that grew out of this effort. The other reports in the series are

- Raphael S. Cohen et al., *The Future of Warfare in 2030: Project Overview and Conclusions* (RR-2849/1-AF)
- Raphael S. Cohen, Eugeniu Han, and Ashley L. Rhoades, *Geopolitical Trends and the Future of Warfare: The Changing Global Environment and Its Implications for the U.S. Air Force* (RR-2849/2-AF)
- Forrest E. Morgan and Raphael S. Cohen, *Military Trends and the Future of Warfare: The Changing Global Environment and Its Implications for the U.S. Air Force* (RR-2849/3-AF)
- Shira Efron, Kurt Klein, and Raphael S. Cohen, *Environment, Geography, and the Future of Warfare: The Changing Global Environment and Its Implications for the U.S. Air Force* (RR-2849/5-AF)
- Bryan Frederick and Nathan Chandler, *Restraint and the Future of Warfare: The Changing Global Environment and Its Implications for the U.S. Air Force* (RR-2849/6-AF).

This volume examines six economic trends by asking four questions. First, what does research say about how this variable shapes the conduct of warfare? Second, how has this variable historically shaped the conduct of warfare, especially in the post–Cold War era? Third, how might this variable be expected to change through 2030? And finally, but perhaps most importantly, how might this variable affect the future of warfare in this time frame, especially as it relates to the U.S. armed forces and the U.S. Air Force in particular? By answering these questions, it is hoped that this report will paint a picture of how economic developments, trends, and disputes will shape conflict over the next decade plus.

This research was sponsored by the Director of Strategy, Concepts and Assessments, Deputy Chief of Staff for Strategic Plans and Requirements (AF/A5S). It is part of a larger study, entitled *The Future of Warfare*, that assists the Air Force in assessing trends in the future strategic environment for the next Air Force strategy. This report should be of value to the national security community and interested members of the general public, especially those with an interest in how global trends will affect the conduct of warfare. Comments are welcome and should be sent to the authors, Howard J. Shatz and Nathan Chandler, or to the project leader, Raphael S. Cohen. Research was completed in October 2018.

RAND Project AIR FORCE

RAND Project AIR FORCE (PAF), a division of the RAND Corporation, is the U.S. Air Force's federally funded research and development center for studies and analyses. PAF provides the Air Force with independent analyses of policy alternatives affecting the development, employment, combat readiness, and support of current and future air, space, and cyber forces. Research is conducted in four programs: Force Modernization and Employment; Manpower, Personnel, and Training; Resource Management; and Strategy and Doctrine. The research reported here was prepared under contract FA7014-16-D-1000.

Additional information about PAF is available on our website: www.rand.org/paf.

This report documents work originally shared with the U.S. Air Force in September 2018. The draft report, issued September 18, 2018, was reviewed by formal peer reviewers and U.S. Air Force subject-matter experts.

Contents

Figures and Tables

Figures

Tables

Summary

Economic developments, trends, and disputes rarely cause wars, but they can affect the risk of war and how wars are fought. This report focuses on six economic trends that could influence the future of war:

1. increasing pressure on the global trading system
2. relative declines in U.S. and allied economic might
3. the rise of China
4. the search for new resources
5. the shrinking defense industrial base
6. the decreasing power of U.S. sanctions.

We consider these issues within roughly a ten-year time frame, through 2030, to coincide with two U.S. Department of Defense planning cycles.

Economic-related risk of major war is rising and expected to continue doing so through 2030; at the same time, economic factors are lowering the ability of the United States and its allies to win such a war decisively. Although the trend lines are negative in terms of both risk and capability, the expected change in future risk levels is small. The United States and its partners likely will remain not only the dominant economic powers through 2030 but also the dominant military powers.

Nonetheless, the economic trends we discuss do elevate the risk of war and could lead to greater U.S. vulnerability. Rising global protectionism and falling support for truly multilateral trade and investment openness increase tensions among nations. The rise of China as an economic power and other changes to the global economy and security environment have introduced new stresses that great powers have not dealt with for generations. Oil has sparked war and will remain important to the global economy. In addition, technological change has increased demand for new resources, and nations are still trying to ensure that they can easily access those resources to fuel their economies; although this demand is unlikely to increase the risk of war, it does increase global economic uncertainty.

Although economic growth in the United States and allied nations will continue, their combined share of the global economy has been falling and is likely to continue doing so while that of competitors or adversaries is likely to rise. As a result, Western powers will have less ability to rely on economic might to support warfighting and to serve as global leaders in a variety of institutions. In addition, these economic changes could lead to decreased ability to use sanctions as a substitute for coercive action, although such a decrease is not yet apparent. Meanwhile, the U.S. and European defense industrial bases have consolidated and military equipment has become far more complex than in the past, reducing the ability to retain redundancy and to surge production.

These economic trends could affect who will fight future wars, as well as how, where, when, and why those wars will be fought. Many of these trends slightly increase the likelihood of great-power war. Only great powers have the ability to raise global trade barriers in a meaningful way, and only other great powers are likely to challenge such actions. If the rise of China threatens to upend the global system, the United States and Japan are most likely to be affected and have the power to take action; Europe likely will be affected, but its willingness to act is uncertain.

Not all of these trends affect great powers. Resource wars generally occur in developing countries as either interstate wars or civil wars. Likewise, any decline in U.S. power might spur challenges by midsize adversaries. How wars will be fought could change as well. With lower resilience and a lower ability to replenish weapons, trends in the defense industrial base suggest that belligerents might strive for a knockout blow or seek to escalate conflict quickly.

All of these trends move slowly. It appears unlikely that they will lead the United States into war any time before 2030, although the likelihood is somewhat higher toward the end of the period. If war should occur as a result of economic developments, trends, or disputes, the reasons will stem largely from fears of global changes that erode a country's growth prospects. This suggests that attempting to force fundamental changes in a country's economic system raises the risk of war. Economic trends could also lead to war as a result of miscalculation—an attack either to take advantage of perceived strength or to act before strength declines. Regardless of cause, location, timing, and reason, any great-power war is likely to cause enormous economic damage.

That developments will lead to higher risk and more vulnerability is highly uncertain, and it is easy to create scenarios that are far more optimistic (new agreements on trade and investment liberalization, productivity revolutions in the United States, Europe, and Japan) or pessimistic (a return to 1930s-style protectionism and a closing off of the world economy). Accordingly, it is also useful for defense planners to consider steps that will strengthen security and their military edge regardless of outcome. Two such steps are of the highest priority for the United States.

The first is to repair and strengthen the U.S. economy, especially its government budget. The U.S. Congressional Budget Office projects that the federal debt held by the public will rise from 78 percent of gross domestic product in 2018 to 99 percent in 2030, the highest level since 1946, when it hit 106 percent in the wake of borrowing to fund World War II. This will constrain military spending, harm the country's ability to prepare for war, and could limit military action in time of security crisis. Furthermore, it will limit the government's ability to respond to and repair the damage from economic and financial crises.

The second is to strengthen global institutional structures that the United States created and still dominates with allies. The security policy of the United States is to work in concert with allies and partners, and global institutions provide an efficient way to do that. Even with the growth of China and the relative decline of Europe and Japan, the United States and its allies combined will be the dominant economies through 2030 and, together, will have the most technologically advanced and diversified military industries. Although the institutional arrangements founded at the end of World War II might need reform, the reasons they were founded still remain: They provide venues for mediating disputes, agreeing to common rules, and generally pursuing joint efforts toward beneficial development where joint efforts are useful. Those reasons are sure to extend through 2030.

Acknowledgments

This study would not have been possible without the help of many people. First and foremost, we thank Brig Gen David Hicks, Col Linc Bonner, and Scott Wheeler of the Air Force A5S for sponsoring this study and guiding it along the way. We also thank Paula Thornhill, the Project Air Force Strategy and Doctrine Program Director, for her guidance and mentorship. The research team owes a special debt of gratitude to numerous experts across the globe who volunteered their time to give their perspectives on economic trends and the future of warfare both within their region and globally. Although human subjects protocol prevents us from thanking them by name, we thank the following institutions for hosting our research visits as part of the overall project: UK Ministry of Defence's Development, Concepts, and Doctrine Centre; UK Parliament, House of Commons Staff; The Royal Institute of International Affairs (Chatham House); Control Risks; Royal United Services Institute for Defence and Security Studies; London School of Economics and Political Science IDEAS; International Institute of Strategic Studies; NATO Headquarters; European Commission; Centre for European Policy Studies; European Centre for International Political Economy; German Federal Ministry of Defence; German Institute for International and Security Affairs (SWP); German Federal Parliament; German Federal Foreign Office; European Council on Foreign Relations; Polish Ministry of Foreign Affairs; Polish Ministry of National Defence; Polish Institute of International Affairs; and Centre for Eastern Studies. Reviews by Frank Camm, Michael J. Meese, and Steven W. Popper improved the manuscript substantially. RAND production editor Julienne Ackerman guided the manuscript through publication,

Arwen Bicknell provided expert copy editing, and Dori Walker designed the cover. All errors of fact and interpretation remain the sole responsibility of the authors.

Abbreviations

AM	additive manufacturing
BAE	British Aerospace Systems
BRI	Belt and Road Initiative
CBO	U.S. Congressional Budget Office
DoD	U.S. Department of Defense
DIB	defense industrial base
EU	European Union
FDI	foreign direct investment
G7	Group of Seven
G-20	Group of 20
GATT	General Agreement on Tariffs and Trade
GDP	gross domestic product
IMF	International Monetary Fund
M&A	mergers and acquisitions
NATO	North Atlantic Treaty Organization
PAF	RAND Project AIR FORCE
PPP	purchasing-power parity
RDT&E	research, development, test, and evaluation
RMB	renminbi
USAF	U.S. Air Force
WTO	World Trade Organization

CHAPTER ONE

Global Economic Trends

Security planners considering the future of warfare face the daunting task of planning for a future they do not know with information they do not have. One way to fill information gaps is to consider broad trends that are likely to unfold, keeping in mind that the unexpected should be expected. This report focuses on six economic trends that could influence the future of war:

1. increasing pressure on the global trading system
2. relative declines in U.S. and allied economic might
3. the rise of China
4. the search for new resources
5. the shrinking defense industrial base (DIB)
6. the decreasing power of U.S. sanctions.

We consider these issues within a roughly ten-year time frame, through 2030, to coincide with two U.S. Department of Defense (DoD) planning cycles as captured in the Pentagon's *Future Years Defense Program* document.[1]

[1] Lynn M. Williams and Heidi M. Peters, "Defense Primer: Future Years Defense Program (FYDP)," Washington, D.C., Congressional Research Service, IF 10831, February 16, 2018.

Higher Risk, Lower Ability

Although economic developments, trends, and disputes are not ordinarily thought of as causes of war, they can influence reasons for going to war and the way that wars are fought and won—or lost. Based on existing literature, the historical track record, and current trends, this report provides evidence that the economic-related risk of major war is rising and will continue to do so through 2030 both because of increasing global protectionism and decreasing support for truly multilateral trade and investment openness and because of the rise of China as an economic power and other changes to the global economy and security environment. Increasing demand for resources used in new technology sectors could introduce uncertainty into markets if those resources become constrained. It is our assessment, however, that this increased risk is still small and other factors are more important, as they almost always have been.[2]

In this environment of slightly increased risk, the ability of the United States to rely on its economic strength to support successful warfighting is declining slightly. Declining economic power—at least in relative terms—also might attract more adventurism on the part of rivals and thus raise the risk of war. Although economic growth will continue in the United States and allied nations, their economies will

---

[2] Companion reports in this series assess many of those other factors. They include Raphael S. Cohen, Nathan Chandler, Shira Efron, Bryan Frederick, Eugeniu Han, Kurt Klein, Forrest Morgan, Ashley L. Rhoades, Howard J. Shatz, and Yuliya Shokh, *The Future of Warfare in 2030: Project Overview and Conclusions*, Santa Monica, Calif.: RAND Corporation, RR-2849/1-AF, 2020; Raphael S. Cohen, Eugeniu Han, and Ashley L. Rhoades, *Geopolitical Trends and the Future of Warfare: The Changing Global Environment and Its Implications for the U.S. Air Force*, Santa Monica, Calif.: RAND Corporation, RR-2849/2-AF, 2020; Forrest E. Morgan and Raphael S. Cohen, *Military Trends and the Future of Warfare: The Changing Global Environment and Its Implications for the U.S. Air Force*, Santa Monica, Calif.: RAND Corporation, RR-2849/3-AF, 2020; Shira Efron, Kurt Klein, and Raphael S. Cohen, *Environment, Geography, and the Future of Warfare: The Changing Global Environment and Its Implications for the U.S. Air Force*, Santa Monica, Calif.: RAND Corporation, RR-2849/5-AF, 2020; and Bryan Frederick and Nathan Chandler, *Restraint and the Future of Warfare: The Changing Global Environment and Its Implications for the U.S. Air Force*, Santa Monica, Calif.: RAND Corporation, RR-2849/6-AF, 2020.

constitute a smaller share of the global economy while growth enjoyed by competitors or adversaries is likely to lead those economies to constitute a larger share of the global economy overall. This means that it will be easier for those competitors or adversaries to increase their share of global defense spending. Another potential outcome of relatively declining economic size could be a decreasing ability to use sanctions as a substitute for coercive action, although such a decrease is not yet apparent. Meanwhile, the U.S. and allied DIBs have consolidated and military equipment has become far more complex than in the past, reducing the ability to retain redundancy and to surge production.

Since World War II, civil wars have been far more frequent than interstate wars, and wars with large-scale direct military confrontations between great powers have been rarer still, with the last one ending in 1953. The Cold War, a confrontation between the United States and the Soviet Union and their respective allies, ended with the dissolution of the Soviet Union in 1991. It involved all instruments of U.S. national power, such as military confrontations (usually through proxies); information operations; diplomacy; and, notably, economics, with the United States using its economic power to create an open global economy for nations that wanted to participate and to outspend the Soviet Union on national defense. Beyond indirect military confrontations with the Soviet Union, the United States has been at war for much of the post–World War II period. As of 2018, the United States participated in numerous conflicts in different ways and is likely to face consequences in the future if there are changes in the risk of war. We judge both the increased risk of major war and the erosion of U.S. and allied dominance to be small. But both are headed in the wrong direction, and that is cause for concern.

Methods and Approach

We selected our six trends based on a review of literature about war and its relationship to economic developments, trends, and disputes; interviews with experts; primacy of trends as defined by DoD, the U.S. Air Force (USAF), and the Donald Trump administration; and guidance by project sponsors in USAF.[3] In analyzing each trend, we drew on available literature, data, and interviews. The literature consisted of published and unpublished academic papers, policy research organization reports, industry reports, trade publications, web posts by experts, and government and multilateral organization publications.[4] Some of the literature, especially the large-scale statistical studies, does not differentiate between smaller interstate wars and great-power wars and so might have fewer implications for the United States. Still, the United States has tended to get involved in a variety of wars and thus could be affected even by smaller interstate wars. Our data sources were the World Bank, North Atlantic Treaty Organization (NATO), the International Monetary Fund (IMF), the Stockholm International Peace Research Institute, and the World Trade Organization, among others. Interviews were conducted largely during the last two weeks of April 2018 in London, Brussels, Berlin, and Warsaw. In those cities, we met

---

[3] Our material on the global trading system came largely from a review of the literature and from interviews. Our material on China came from interviews and from previous work that the RAND Corporation has done on the issue. Our material on resources came from the literature and new attention from the Trump administration, particularly Presidential Executive Order 13817 (White House, *A Federal Strategy to Ensure Secure and Reliable Supplies of Critical Minerals*, Washington, D.C.: Executive Order 13817, December 20, 2017c, via *Federal Register*, Vol. 82, No. 246, December 26, 2017, pp. 60835–60837). Our material on sanctions came largely from previous work that RAND has done on the issue and a review of the literature. Our material on the relative size of the United States and its allies in the global economy came from previous work that RAND has done, a review of the literature and data, and interviews. Finally, our material on the DIB came from discussions with the sponsor and from attention to the issue by DoD, USAF, and the administration, as recognized in Executive Order 13806. White House, *Assessing and Strengthening the Manufacturing and Defense Industrial Base and Supply Chain Resiliency of the United States*, Washington, D.C.: Executive Order 13806, July 21, 2017a.

[4] The literature fits within the broad topic of the effects of economics on military affairs, an area of research within what is known as *peace economics*. In the early 2000s, two economists specializing in peace economics outlined topics needing more research, some of which are mentioned in this report (Dietrich Fischer and Jurgen Brauer, "Twenty Questions for Peace Economics: A Research Agenda," *Defence and Peace Economics*, Vol. 14, No. 3, 2003). Peace economics has been defined as economic research that "focuses upon the causes of conflict and ways that it can be managed, reduced, or eliminated." Charles Anderton, "Economic Theorizing of Conflict: Historical Contributions, Future Possibilities," *Defence and Peace Economics*, Vol. 14, No. 3, 2003.

with officials from different Ministries of Foreign Affairs and Defense, the European Commission, parliaments, and NATO. We also met with researchers from policy research organizations oriented to international affairs, security, and economics.

In the remainder of this report, we discuss each trend.[5] For each trend, we first provide an introduction that describes the line of argument the chapter will take and summarizes what the published literature says. We then report how the trend has influenced war in the past and speculate on how it might evolve in the future. We conclude each chapter with a discussion of implications for the future of warfare and for USAF. In the final chapter, we offer an overview of how these trends shed light on who might fight future wars, and how, where, when and why they might fight. The answers are necessarily incomplete, and we conclude with a short section on potential surprises and preparing for them.

War is often thought of as military action, but conflict and actions to shape or forestall potential conflicts go beyond that definition. Conflict can include the use of economics to shape the behavior of an adversary and the use of economic and financial actions to punish a target or to conduct economic warfare against that target. Conducting war and shaping the environment before and during military conflict can also include the use of diplomacy, information operations, intelligence, and law enforcement. Accordingly, in discussing the implications of economic trends for the future of warfare, we take a broader view than just military action.

---

[5] Demographic change will influence many of these trends. For more information, see Martin C. Libicki, Howard J. Shatz, and Julie E. Taylor, *Global Demographic Change and Its Implications for Military Power*, Santa Monica, Calif.: RAND Corporation, MG-1091-AF, 2011.

CHAPTER TWO

Trend 1: Increasing Pressure on the Global Trading System

The 21st-century global economy is far more open to international trade and investment than it was for most of the 20th century. Policy changes and technological advancements have made it easy to move goods, services, and capital to other countries, and nearly every country has come to ascribe to a common set of international trade rules since the end of the Cold War.

Although the global trading system is far more open than it has been for most of the past 100 years, it has come under pressure since the global financial crisis of 2008. In November of that year, during the crisis, the G-20 governments agreed to a standstill on protectionist measures and committed to refraining from raising new barriers to trade and investment.[1] Since that time, however, the G-20 governments around the world have instituted more than 12,000 trade-related interventions that have discriminated against foreign commercial interests and only about 4,500 that have liberalized market access or benefited

[1] Barbara Barone and Robert Bendini, *Protectionism in the G20 (2015)*, Policy Department, General-Directorate for External Policies, European Parliament, DG EXPO/B/PolDep/Note/2015_136, March 2015. G-20 refers to "Group of 20," an international forum for the governments and central bank governors from Argentina, Australia, Brazil, Canada, China, the European Union, France, Germany, India, Indonesia, Italy, Japan, Mexico, Russia, Saudi Arabia, South Africa, South Korea, Turkey, the United Kingdom, and the United States. Spain is a permanent guest invitee.

foreign commercial interests. In fact, in every year since the crisis, more than 70 percent of trade interventions have been harmful.[2]

World Trade Organization (WTO) members ended the Doha Round multilateral trade negotiations in 2015 without a successful conclusion. This did not cause greater restraints in the global economy, but it was the first time in the history of the WTO and its predecessor, the General Agreement on Tariffs and Trade (GATT), that a major multilateral trade liberalization negotiating round failed.[3] In the spring of 2018, new steel and aluminum tariffs levied by the United States, retaliation by various trading partners, and tariffs on China levied by the United States and subsequent Chinese retaliation all led to further pressure on the normal operations of the global trading system.[4]

In this chapter, we discuss three related aspects of trade and war: (1) general findings about the relationship between trade and war; (2) the overall rules and norms related to trade; and (3) the institutional underpinnings of the global trading system, specifically the WTO. In addition to trade, we include other forms of international economic exchange.

---

[2] Global Trade Alert, "Interventions per Year," online spreadsheet, undated. See also Simon J. Evenett and Johannes Fritz, *Going Spare: Steel, Excess Capacity, and Protectionism*, London: CEPR Press, 22nd Global Trade Alert Report, 2018. The Global Trade Alert project identifies nine broad categories of trade-related interventions, within which are 56 subcategories. Examples of these subcategories are controls on credit operations, export quotas, import tariffs, and entry and ownership rules for foreign direct investment. Simon J. Evenett and Johannes Fritz, *The Global Trade Alert Database Handbook*, St. Gallen, Switzerland, March 28, 2018b.

[3] Shawn Donnan, "Trade Talks Lead to 'Death of Doha and Birth of New WTO," *Financial Times*, December 20, 2015. The WTO and the GATT have conducted nine negotiation rounds with the aim of multilateral trade liberalization covering all member countries. The Doha Round, also known as the Doha Development Agenda, was the latest round and started in November 2001. WTO, "The GATT Years: From Havana to Marrakech," webpage, undated-c; WTO, "The Doha Round," webpage, undated-b.

[4] There was widespread global support for some type of action related to China. For example, the Group of Seven (G7; Canada, France, Germany, Italy, Japan, the United Kingdom, and the United States) communique from the Charlevoix meeting (not endorsed by the United States) called for "new rules where needed to foster a truly level playing field, addressing in particular non-market oriented policies and practices, and inadequate protection of intellectual property rights, such as forced technology transfer or cyber-enabled theft," a statement that can refer only to China. Group of Seven, "The Charlevoix G7 Summit Communique," Charlevoix, Quebec, June 9, 2018.

Context: Bilateral Trade, Lower Conflict Risk

There is a long-held belief that freer global trade leads to less war. As early as the 18th century, free trade was theorized to be one element in a more peaceful world. (Another element was representative government, considered important because although authoritarian or absolute rulers might profit from the conquest of territory, most citizens under such rule would be unlikely to see a direct benefit.[5]) The core argument regarding trade was that if people could trade freely for goods and services, there would be no need to conquer territory to gain them. Moreover, trade creates interdependencies that make war more costly. Some early economists recognized that trade could be related to the occurrence of war, noting that the mercantilist view (in which one nation gains in trade what another loses) could lead to attempts to control resources and foreign markets. However, they also emphasized that this view was a misconception of trade.[6]

Modern analysis has provided support for the free-trade hypothesis on its own and for the hypothesis that combines benefits of free trade and representative government.[7] For example, one general finding has been that the level of international trade and the probability of many types of wars are inversely related. However, statistical studies that include numerous countries over long periods of time show that the relationship is more complicated than simply one of more trade resulting in fewer wars.

The clearest result is that more *bilateral* trade is, in fact, related to a lower risk of conflict. Based on a data set of more than

---

[5] Ludwig von Mises, "The Economic Causes of War," lecture delivered in Orange County, California, in October 1944, reprinted in *The Freeman*, April 2004; John R. Oneal, Frances H. Oneal, Zeev Maoz, and Bruce Russett, "The Liberal Peace: Interdependence, Democracy, and International Conflict, 1950–1985," *Journal of Peace Research*, Vol. 33, No. 1, February 1996. Von Mises argued that two conditions were necessary: free trade and representative government. Under representative government, people would be less inclined to support wars because they would not directly benefit.

[6] Anderton, 2003.

[7] Edward D. Mansfield, *Power, Trade, and War*, Princeton, N.J.: Princeton University Press, 1994.

14,000 country-pairs from 1950 to 2000 (for a total data set of more than 290,000 observations), one analysis found that bilateral trade dependence significantly reduces the probability of conflict, especially for nearby countries.[8] Using similar data (with a total data set of 536,000 observations) but different methods, another analysis found that if the world were to return to the level of bilateral trade in 1970—much lower than in 2000—the probability of conflict would be 8 percent to 15 percent higher for countries up to 5,000 kilometers from each other.[9]

Research that considers both bilateral trade and *multilateral* trade found different effects, but there is disagreement over these effects. For example, one analysis found that greater multilateral openness reduces the chance of conflict and does so more strongly for countries with greater distance between them.[10] In contrast, a separate analysis found that greater multilateral trade openness tends to increase the probability of conflict between any two countries (while finding that bilateral trade reduces conflict).[11] The authors attributed the multilateral effect to the idea that if a country is more open to the world as a whole, the loss of trade with a single bilateral partner is felt less and thus the loss from conflict is less than it might be otherwise.

---

[8] Jong-Wha Lee and Ju Hyun Pyun, *Does Trade Integration Contribute to Peace?* Mandaluyong, Philippines: Asian Development Bank, Working Paper Series on Regional Integration No. 24, January 2009. The authors established the causal pathway from increased trade to reduced conflict in two ways in the statistical analysis. First, they lagged the trade variables by three years, so that whatever conflict occurrence they analyzed appeared well after trade took place. However, trade aggregates tend to be persistent, so they also implemented what is known as an instrumental variables approach, an accepted method of determining causality.

[9] Philippe Martin, Thierry Mayer, and Mathias Thoenig, "Make Trade Not War?" *The Review of Economic Studies*, Vol. 75, 2008. The authors established the causal pathway from trade to conflict by controlling for variables that affect both conflict and trade; by including variables to control for events that are common to all countries at one time or events that are common to pairs of countries at all times; and by implementing what is known as an instrumental variables approach, an accepted method of determining causality.

[10] Lee and Pyun, 2009.

[11] Martin, Mayer, and Thoenig, 2008. Lee and Pyun, 2009, wrote that this is because of the type of model chosen by Martin, Mayer, and Thoenig.

Most research on economic interdependence and war focuses on trade, but research on investment also exists. One study reported a two-way relationship between conflict and *foreign direct investment* (FDI), defined as cross-border investment for the purpose of controlling a business. Greater international cooperation, or decreased international conflict, leads to increases in FDI. At the same time, increases in FDI among pairs of countries reduce conflict between those countries.[12]

The mechanism by which increased trade—at least, bilateral trade—leads to decreased probability of conflict is not fully understood. It might not even be an effect of more trade per se; rather, it might be an effect of the *expectation* of more trade. One review examined 30 instances of great-power war from 1791 to 1990 in which economic interdependence played a role and found that the expectation of declining trade and investment opportunities was a source of tension in all of them. In a subset, other economic motivations were also present, such as risks and benefits of economic entanglement.[13]

Modern research has also identified several other ways that economic developments, trends, and disputes are related to war. When partner countries are highly developed and have good contract enforcement (so that disputes can be settled in a fair manner), more trade dependence is related to a lower probability of conflict. The chance of conflict increases in the presence of protectionism and higher levels of state control of the economy.[14]

---

[12] Solomon Polachek, Carlos Seiglie, and Jun Xiang, "The Impact of Foreign Direct Investment on International Conflict," *Defence and Peace Economics*, Vol. 18, No. 5, 2007.

[13] The finding is attributed to Dale C. Copeland, *Economic Interdependence and War*, Princeton, N.J.: Princeton University Press, 2015, in Massimo Morelli and Tommaso Sonno, "On Economic Interdependence and War," *Journal of Economic Literature*, Vol. 55, No. 3, 2017.

[14] Morelli and Sonno, 2017.

Historical Trend: Declining Trade Barriers, Rising World Trade and Investment

Causes of war are highly complex and often numerous, but there is evidence that expectations of being cut off from markets have led to conflict. A series of lectures held just before the outbreak of World War II presented an analysis of economic causes of war that identified rising barriers to trade and investment as contributors to World War I, to Japanese militarism, and to the brewing European conflict.[15] Increasing state control of several economies (particularly those of Germany and the Soviet Union) was also identified as a contributor to conflict because of the direct link between performance of enterprises and state power.

Since World War II, trade barriers have fallen, and trade and investment volumes have risen dramatically. There are few good measures for trade barriers in the immediate postwar period: For world-average tariffs, estimates range from 22 percent to 40 percent.[16] By the 2010s, the world average tariff applied by all countries was 9 percent and the rate applied by developed countries—essentially, the countries from which the data used for the immediate post–World War II average were drawn—was 5 percent for all goods and 2.8 percent for non-agricultural goods.[17]

Related to this decline in barriers has been a concomitant rise in world trade and investment. Global merchandise exports in nominal terms increased from $58.5 billion in 1948 to $17.7 trillion in 2017.[18] However, there was also inflation during this period, so these figures overstate trade volumes. An alternative way to consider the growth of nominal trade is to compare it with nominal world income in the form of gross domestic product (GDP). Global merchandise

---

[15] Lionel Robbins, *The Economic Causes of War*, New York: Howard Fertig, 1968.

[16] Chad P. Brown and Douglas A. Irwin, *The GATT's Starting Point: Tariff Levels Circa 1947*, Cambridge, Mass.: National Bureau of Economic Research, NBER Working Paper 21782, December 2015.

[17] WTO, *World Trade Report 2013: Factors Shaping the Future of World Trade*, Geneva, 2013; WTO, "Trade and Tariffs: Trade Grows as Tariffs Decline," Geneva, brochure, 2015a.

[18] WTO, "Statistics on Merchandise Trade," online database, undated-e.

exports rose from 9.6 percent of global GDP in 1960 to 22 percent in 2017, peaking at 25.5 percent in 2008.[19] Global inward *FDI stock*, defined as the cumulative amount of annual FDI, increased from $701 billion in nominal terms in 1980 to $26.7 trillion in 2016.[20] Compared with global GDP, FDI rose from 6.3 percent in 1980 to a peak of 35.2 percent in 2016. Along with falling barriers, other factors contributed to these increases, such as growth of the world economy; changes in technology; changes in shipping, especially the rise of the shipping container; and changes in methods of doing business, especially the development of production-sharing.

Future Projection: Reduced Trade Liberalization and a Weaker WTO

There are several risks to the world trading system. First, the desire for freer trade and investment could be waning. Among developed countries, trade barriers on goods are quite low, so there is little room to continue liberalizing that area of the economy.[21] This means that real benefits of continued trade liberalization for goods will come from liberalizing the trade of developing countries, and they have proven resis-

---

[19] The WTO does compute trade volume indices for a shorter period, but there are flaws, such as differences in product coverage from the value indices on which they are based (WTO, *WTO Statistics Data Sets—Metadata*, undated-g). Nonetheless, the WTO volume indices show that world exports more than doubled between 1980 and the peak year of 2011 but have fallen back since then, with trade volumes 68.7 percent higher in 2017 than in 1980. In contrast, world real GDP grew by 144 percent between 1980 and 2011, and by 187 percent between 1980 and 2017. WTO, undated-e; and World Bank, World Development Indicators, November 14, 2018.

[20] United Nations Conference on Trade and Development, "Foreign Direct Investment: Inward and Outward Flows and Stock, Annual, 1970–2016," database, undated. Note that the trade data reflect a flow, or the new, incremental amount each year, and trade flows are relatively stable. The FDI data are a stock, or cumulative amount over many years. FDI flows, the incremental amount invested each year are highly volatile and serve less well as indicators of trends than do FDI stocks. FDI stock data are unavailable for years before 1980.

[21] Daniel Gros, "Globalisation: The Hype, the Reality, and the Causes of the Recent Slowdown in Global Trade," VOX: CEPR Policy Portal, June 30, 2017.

tant. Because these countries are growing faster than the developed countries, overall global liberalization could actually decrease over time.

Second, given the difficulties in bringing about freer goods trade, it is possible that liberalization of trade in services could give global trading a boost. But services liberalization might involve benefits to large technology companies with low numbers of employees, with the result that this approach would have only limited support. Services liberalization also could involve changes in domestic regulations rather than tariffs, which also might limit popular support.[22]

Third, the main trading institution might be weakening. Global governance of trade now rests with the WTO. Although it was founded in 1995, it has its roots in the GATT, which went into effect in 1947 and lasted until the end of 1994 before being incorporated into the WTO.[23] As of July 29, 2016, the organization had 164 members, accounting for nearly all of global trade, and 23 observer governments.[24]

The main roles of the WTO are to liberalize trade in all its forms through trade negotiations; ensure implementation of trade agreements through monitoring; conduct binding dispute settlement; help build trade capacity in developing countries; and conduct outreach with all trade stakeholders, such as governments, international organizations,

---

[22] These observations stem from interviews with government officials and researchers in London and Brussels in April 2018. Barriers to trade in goods have traditionally, although not exclusively, been tariffs, a form of taxation. These can be changed and have little direct effect on the majority of a country's population, except for the sectors competing directly with the foreign sector subject to tariffs. Services trade barriers, in contrast, are often regulatory, and services trade liberalization could affect regulatory autonomy and be more politically sensitive than tax rate changes. For sensitivities regarding regulation and services trade, see Bernard Hoekman and Aaditya Matoo, *Services Trade Liberalization and Regulatory Reform: Re-Invigorating International Competition*, Washington, D.C.: World Bank, Policy Research Working Paper 5517, January 2011; and United Nations Conference on Trade and Development Secretariat, *Services, Development and Trade: The Regulatory and Institutional Dimension*, Geneva, Switzerland, TD/B/C.I/MEM.4/11, March 9, 2016.

[23] Craig VanGrasstek, *The History and Future of the World Trade Organization*, Geneva: World Trade Organization, 2013.

[24] WTO, "Members and Observers," webpage, undated-d.

the media, and the general public.[25] Notably, one of the major changes in the shift from the GATT to the WTO was the creation of binding dispute settlement. Although there are numerous trade agreements, the WTO sets the standards, and all trade agreements are designed to conform to WTO rules. As a result, the WTO is the foundation of the rules-based international trading system. However, this foundation is now under threat.

Japan and U.S. European allies have become particularly concerned about the future of the world trading system.[26] The European Union (EU) favors institutions and rules within which it can operate but saw flagging U.S. support for the WTO (at least, in early 2018). Some in Europe view such economic institutions as part of a broader package shoring up the overall international order. Europeans involved in international policy are divided as to whether Europe is strong enough to maintain the WTO if the United States does not support it. And the WTO might be weakening even beyond the issue of U.S. support. The failure of the Doha Development Agenda multilateral trade round and the prospects of no further rounds through the early 2020s (and perhaps beyond) have limited the WTO's role in large-scale trade liberalization efforts, one of its main reasons for being. Although Europeans express strong support for the WTO, they also say they believe that it cannot solve all the challenges of the global trading system.

Finally, the issue of U.S. support for the WTO brings up a related issue: whether any major economy will want to serve as the prime supporter of the global trading system in the future if the United States chooses not to. The United States was the leader in setting up the post–World War II trading system; it played a central role in the Uruguay Round negotiations that started the WTO; and it was the moving force (with the EU) behind the start of the Doha Round.[27] In the extreme, the United States could exit the WTO. As of late 2018, that seemed

---

[25] WTO, "What We Do," webpage, undated-f.

[26] These observations stem from interviews with government officials and researchers in London, Brussels, Berlin, and Warsaw in April 2018.

[27] Kevin Buterbaugh and Richard Fulton, *The WTO Primer: Tracing Trade's Visible Hand Through Case Studies*, New York: Palgrave MacMillan, 2007.

unlikely, although not impossible. Alternatively, the United States might choose not to push for more liberalization, or it might push to adjust trade rules in response to changes in the global economy, which could be tantamount to decreasing liberalization. The levels of trade by the United States, China, and the EU are all of similar magnitude, so there is no clear leader for trade liberalization. The EU and China are both stronger supporters of trade institutions; the EU and the United States are more aligned on commercial issues, meaning they are both advocates for high levels of economic openness (at least as of mid-2018).

These factors suggest a period of drift for the global trading system. Companies will continue to trade because there is benefit to doing so. But major liberalization efforts might be stalled, and trade rules might not adapt to new developments in technology and the economy.

Implications for the U.S. Air Force and the Future of Warfare

The world has seen deep trade liberalization and increasingly high levels of interdependence since the end of World War II. Failures to advance in most of the remaining issues of trade liberalization—such as the further lowering of barriers to goods trade, services liberalization, and responding to changes in trade wrought by technological developments—do not necessarily amount to a reversal of trade liberalization. International commitment to trade and interdependence as they exist now is significant and deep. Current negotiations in reaction to domestic political pressure are largely on the margins of an overall existing liberal international trading system. However, interviews with numerous officials suggest concern about both popular and political support for the current order. Furthermore, liberalization will take small steps backward in the absence of further agreements as economies change and a larger share of economic activity is not covered by international trade rules.

Disruptions in the international trading system are unlikely to be direct causes of war, but they can increase international tension, however small such an increase might be. Historically, countries have tried to take action when trading opportunities were seen to diminish to avoid poorer economic performance and subsequent risks of domestic unrest or dissatisfaction. The WTO provides one venue for such action through its dispute resolution mechanism, but that is not operating as well as in the recent past, thus diminishing this avenue for easing trade tensions.

There is little that DoD can do to shape the global economy. Still, these trends call for DoD and USAF to increase their monitoring of the global economic environment, such as the increase of trade barriers, the effects of these barriers on potential U.S. adversaries and allies, and the policy measures being taken in response to these barriers. Beyond such monitoring, DoD and USAF also might increase efforts at military cooperation to compensate for less-robust economic relations and help maintain international relationships. Military-to-military contacts, joint exercises, and other DoD programs could relieve some stress in international relations that is caused by increasing pressure in the global trading system.

CHAPTER THREE

Trend 2: Relative Declines in U.S. and Allied Economic Might

Economic relations can affect a nation's reasons for going to war. The wealth and output generated by economic activity also can influence warfighting and military victory directly by funding the personnel, equipment, and operations of the armed forces and the technological development that can lead to more lethal weapons.

The United States is at the head of what is not only the mightiest military alliance but also the richest. In 2017, the United States and its treaty allies accounted for 57.9 percent of world nominal GDP at market exchange rates.[1] The 2017 *National Security Strategy of the United States* identifies four countries as challengers to the United States and the global order—China, Russia, Iran, and North Korea.[2] Data for North Korea are not available, but the other three countries accounted for 18.2 percent of global GDP in 2017.[3]

It is true that the size of the overall economy does not necessarily translate into military expenditures; countries might spend more or less of their total income on their armed forces, depending on their priorities. In this case, the United States and its allies are spending

---

[1] World Bank, 2018. Treaty allies as of 2018 consist of the 28 non-U.S. NATO members as of July 2018, Australia, Korea, Japan, New Zealand, the Philippines, and Thailand.

[2] White House, *National Security Strategy of the United States*, Washington, D.C., December 2017b.

[3] These figures include Hong Kong and Macao in the China total based on the assumption that if China were to enter a conflict, it would draw on the resources of those two Special Administrative Regions as needed.

more in aggregate than their challengers—in 2017, they accounted for 62.2 percent of total military spending, compared with 17.8 percent for the challengers.[4] This could overcount the expenditures of the allies and undercount the expenditures of the challengers in some ways; a large portion of military spending is personnel, and personnel costs are likely higher for Western allies. Still, even after a personnel adjustment, Western allied military spending would still be higher than that of the challengers. We discuss this adjustment further when we discuss future projections.

With few exceptions, such as 2009, the global economy is continuously growing. If the global economy were to be considered a pie, every year the size of the overall pie is getting larger. But countries grow at different rates. Developing countries, including China, tend to grow more rapidly than more economically advanced countries. Advanced countries, including the United States and EU members, tend to grow more slowly for a variety of reasons. Consequently, while all tend to grow, their *relative* size in the global economy changes, with that of the developing countries getting larger and that of the advanced countries getting smaller.

The global share of GDP accounted for by the United States and its allies is decreasing while the global share of GDP accounted for by U.S. challengers is trending up. This increased share is largely because of China, with other challengers either growing slowly or starting from very low levels of GDP.[5] But the shift in the global

---

[4] Data for NATO members are from NATO, "Defence Expenditures of NATO Countries (2010–2017)," Brussels, press release, Communique PR/CP (2018) 16, March 15, 2018a. Data for non-NATO members are from Stockholm International Peace Research Institute, "SIPRI Military Expenditure Database 2018," Solna, Sweden, undated. Data for the Western allies do not include Iceland. Data for the challengers do not include North Korea and might not include Hong Kong or Macao.

[5] The share of the global economy accounted for by countries that are neither allies nor challengers is also growing. For example, in 1990, India accounted for 1.4 percent of world nominal GDP. In 2017, it accounted for 3.2 percent (World Bank, 2018).

source of economic output could have implications for future military power and warfighting ability.[6]

Context: "Rich Nation, Strong Army"

Spending on the armed forces does not correlate perfectly with effective armed forces, but there is good evidence that the two are related. Both World War I and World War II offer several lessons on the relationship between economic size and military victory.[7] In both wars, the side that deployed the most warfighters and equipment won, even if some components of each side floundered. For example, in World War I, the allied powers mobilized 41 million soldiers, compared with 26 million for the central powers, and the allied powers produced 125,000 aircraft and 8,900 tanks, compared with 47,000 aircraft and 100 tanks for the central powers.[8] What made this possible was the prewar GDP of each side; the sizes of their economies were more important than territory or population sizes. More money also provided a cushion for wartime errors. This success is conditional on time and geography, however. A quick, successful strike by an aggressor would limit or perhaps completely halt the richer, defending country's ability to mobilize resources and respond to errors in strategy.

Economic size affects the outcomes of more than just modern, global wars. Examples throughout history indicate that economic might, although certainly not determinative, can aid in military victory.[9] The industrial strength of the North in the U.S. Civil War eventually helped in achieving victory over the Confederate States. The Meiji Japanese

---

6 Martin C. McGuire, "Economics of Defense in a Globalized World," in Todd Sandler and Keith Hartley, eds., *Handbook of Defense Economics*, Vol. 2, Amsterdam: Elsevier B.V., 2007, Chapter 21, pp. 623–648.

7 This draws from Mark Harrison, *The Economics of Conflict and Coercion*, Singapore: World Scientific, 2014.

8 Harrison, 2014.

9 Christian P. Potholm, *Winning at War: Seven Keys to Military Victory Throughout History*, Lanham, Md.: Rowman & Littlefield, 2010.

saying "rich nation, strong army" also reflects this relationship.[10] Along with economic size, the overall level of economic development as reflected by per capita GDP appears to be related to success in military conflict. An analysis of hundreds of battles and wars between 1898 and 1987 found that the side with the higher level of economic development consistently outfought its opponents.[11] Economic development brings several benefits. Most important, it provides an advantage in producing better military equipment and better-trained military personnel.[12]

Historical Trend: Declining U.S.–Allies Share of Global Economy

The United States and its treaty allies constitute an overwhelming share of the global economy when measured at market exchange rates (Figure 3.1). But this has been declining. In 1990, the United States and its 2018 treaty allies—many of which were not treaty allies in 1990 and some of which were, in fact, adversaries—accounted for 78.2 per-

[10] As cited in Potholm, 2010.

[11] Michael Beckley, "Economic Development and Military Effectiveness," *Journal of Strategic Studies*, Vol. 33, No. 1, February 2010. The specific test was of a variable called the loss-exchange ratio, the attacker's casualties divided by the defender's casualties, and the determinant being tested was the relative per capita GDPs. In a sample of 223 events, when the attacker's per capita GDP was higher, the defender suffered more casualties relative to the attacker. This is true even after taking defense spending into account. Additional variables included in the statistical test were a democracy indicator, human capital, two measures of civil-military relations, a series of cultural indicators, military spending per soldier, total troop strength, number of tanks, ground-attack aircraft sorties, and number of artillery tubes engaged.

[12] Perhaps of concern to the United States, one study found that greater economic equality is positively related to victory in war (James K. Galbraith, Corwin Priest, and George Purcell, "Economic Equality and Victory in War: An Empirical Investigation," *Defence and Peace Economics*, Vol. 18, No. 5, 2007). Among developed countries, the EU and Japan tend to have greater equality after taxes and transfers; the United States tends to be more unequal. When factoring in developing countries, China is even more unequal.

Figure 3.1
Share of Nominal World GDP Produced by the United States, Allies, and Challengers

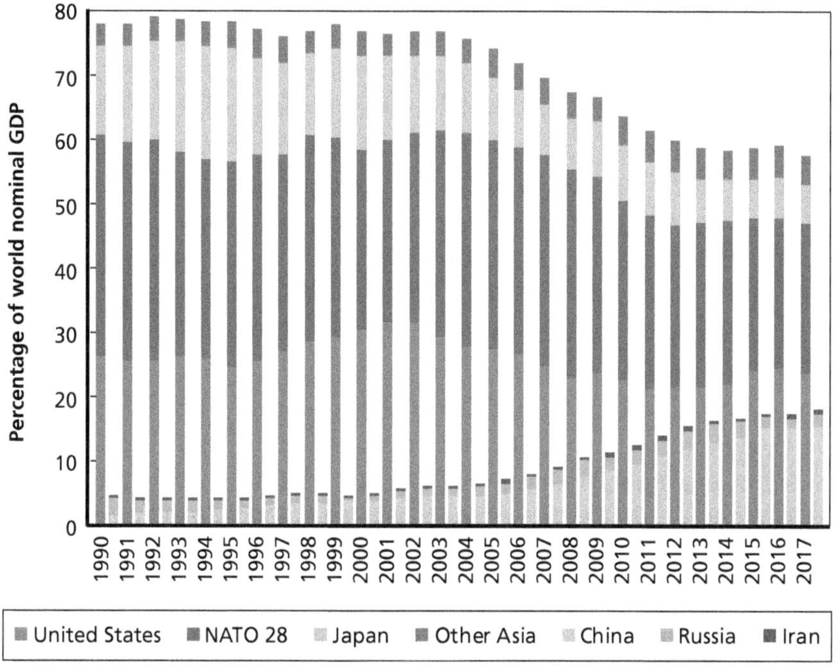

SOURCE: World Bank, 2018.
NOTES: GDP is in terms of nominal U.S. dollars converted at market exchange rates. "NATO 28" = the 28 non-U.S. NATO members as of July 2018; "Other Asia" = U.S. treaty allies Australia, Korea, New Zealand, Philippines, and Thailand; "China" = China, Hong Kong, and Macao, because even though the jurisdictions are under the one country–two systems model, it is likely that China would draw on Hong Kong and Macao as needed in wartime. The 2017 *National Security Strategy of the United States* identified China, Russia, Iran, and North Korea as challengers to the United States and its allies and to the global order (White House, 2017b). No GDP data were available for North Korea.

cent of global GDP.[13] By 2017, this had fallen to 57.9 percent. Of the four countries identified as challengers in the 2017 *National Security*

---

[13] Using only the countries that were treaty allies in 1990 would make the figure 77.4 percent, not much different (World Bank, 2018). Treaty allies as of 2018 include the 28 non-U.S. NATO members as of July 2018, Australia, Korea, Japan, New Zealand, the Philippines, and Thailand.

Strategy of the United States—China, Russia, Iran, and North Korea—the three with available data represented only a tiny portion of world output, 4.8 percent, in 1990. By 2017, this had risen to 18.2 percent.[14]

This decline can be contrasted with the economic disparity between the United States and its allies on the one hand and their adversaries, the Warsaw Pact nations, on the other during the late Cold War period (Figure 3.2). In 1980, after the stagnation of the Soviet economy was well under way, the United States and its allies, including NATO (which was then made up of 14 other nations), accounted for 63.3 percent of the global economy at nominal market exchange rates (Figure 3.2, Panel A).[15] In contrast, the Warsaw Pact nations accounted for only 10.1 percent of world GDP. China, not considered an adversary or competitor at that time, constituted only 2.5 percent of global GDP.

By 1989, the final full year before countries started to leave the Warsaw Pact, the imbalance had grown. The United States and its allies constituted almost 75 percent of global GDP, whereas the Warsaw Pact nations constituted less than 6 percent (Figure 3.2, Panel B). The United States and its allies maintained a share of greater than 75 percent of the global economy through 2004.

Returning to the post–Cold War era, it is useful to disaggregate how the shares have changed since 1990. Within the U.S. alliance structure, the U.S. share of global GDP declined 2.5 percentage points between 1990 and 2017, with all of this decline occurring between 2000 and 2010, the decade that saw the bursting of the dot-com and housing bubbles and the onset of the Great Recession and Global Financial Crisis. The rest of NATO lost 11.2 percentage points, mostly during the 1990s and after 2010. Where the rest of NATO once had a higher GDP than the United States, it ended with a lower one. Japan lost 7.9 percentage points off a smaller base—in 1990, it accounted for 13.9 percent of

---

[14] These figures include Hong Kong and Macao in the China total based on the assumption that if China were to enter a conflict, it would draw on the resources of those two Special Administrative Regions as needed.

[15] For information about the stagnation of the Soviet economy during this period, see Mark Harrison, "Economic Growth and Slowdown," in Edwin Bacon and Mark Sandle, eds., *Brezhnev Reconsidered*, London and Basingstoke: Palgrave, 2002.

Figure 3.2
Share of Nominal World GDP Produced by the United States, Allies, and Challengers During the Cold War

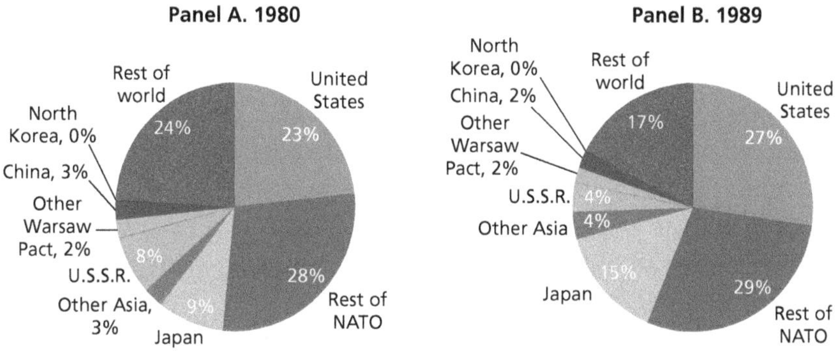

SOURCES: Federal Reserve Bank of St. Louis, "Germany/U.S. Foreign Exchange Rate (DISCONTINUED) [EXGEUS]," undated; U.S. Department of State, Office of the Historian, Bureau of Public Affairs, "The Warsaw Treaty Organization, 1955," webpage, undated; Organisation for Economic Co-operation and Development, *OECD Economic Surveys 1981–1982: Germany*, Paris, June 1982; Irwin L. Collier, *The Estimation of Gross Domestic Product and Its Growth Rate for the German Democratic Republic*, Washington, D.C.: World Bank, Staff Working Papers Number 773, November 1985; Organisation for Economic Co-operation and Development, *OECD Economic Surveys: Germany 1990/1991*, Paris, 1991; United Nations, "National Accounts Main Aggregates Database," online database, December 2017; NATO, "Member Countries," webpage, March 26, 2018b.
NOTES: GDP is in terms of nominal U.S. dollars converted at market exchange rates. "Rest of NATO" = 14 non-U.S. NATO members as of 1980 and 15 non-U.S. NATO members as of 1989; "Other Asia" = U.S. treaty allies Australia, Korea, New Zealand, the Philippines, and Thailand. "China" excludes Hong Kong and Macao because they were not part of the People's Republic during those years. The Warsaw Pact, properly the Warsaw Treaty Organization, encompasses Albania, Bulgaria, the former Czechoslovakia, the former German Democratic Republic (East Germany), Hungary, Poland, and Romania.

the global economy, but by 2017, that figure was only 6.0 percent. The rest of the countries in the U.S. alliance system increased their share of the global economy by 1.4 percentage points.

Among the challengers, China is the major story. China's share of the global economy increased 13.7 percentage points between 1990 and 2017, with most of this share growth coming after 2000. Both Russia's and Iran's declined. We discuss China at length in Chapter Four.

The research cited here points to the importance of not only GDP but of per capita GDP as an indicator of military strength. China has also excelled in that measure of income. Between 1990 and 2017, China's real per capita GDP grew by 8.9 percent per year, the second fastest rate in the world (behind only that of tiny Equatorial Guinea). In contrast, U.S. real per capita GDP grew by 1.4 percent per year (just below the United Kingdom, at almost 1.5 percent, but slightly above Germany, at just below 1.4 percent, and well above France at 1.0 percent, Japan at 0.9 percent, and Italy at 0.5 percent).[16] However, China remains much poorer than the United States. Whereas China's per capita GDP in 1990 was only 1.3 percent of that of the United States as measured by market exchange rates, it had risen by 2017 to 14.8 percent—$8,800 in nominal terms compared with $59,500 for the United States.

To this point, we have compared economies based on nominal market exchange rates. Another way to consider economies is with exchange rates adjusted for purchasing-power parity (PPP), which takes account of different prices in a national economy. Nontraded goods, such as haircuts, are usually priced far lower in developing economies than in developed ones. However, every economy still has to pay market prices for goods that are internationally traded. To calculate PPP-adjusted economic data, the International Comparison Program creates a basket of goods, finds the price of that basket in each economy, then creates an exchange rate based on those basket prices compared with the basket price in U.S. dollars.[17] Typically, because of the low prices of nontradable items in developing economies, this increases the size of developing economies compared with their size at market exchange rates. There are several liabilities to using PPP-adjusted rates, the most important of which are the quality of historical estimates, the use of extrapolation between years in which data are collected, and missing observations.[18]

---

[16] World Bank, 2018.

[17] International Comparison Program, *Purchasing Power Parities and the Real Size of World Economies: A Comprehensive Report of the 2011 International Comparison Program*, Washington, D.C.: World Bank, 2015.

[18] Tim Callen, "PPP Versus the Market: Which Weight Matters?" *Finance & Development*, Vol. 44, No. 1, March 2007.

On the basis of nominal PPP-adjusted GDP, the United States constituted only 15.2 percent of the global economy in 2017, compared with 18.3 percent for China. The Western alliance, including NATO, Japan, and other Asian allies, accounted for 42.4 percent, well ahead of the 23 percent accounted for by China, Hong Kong, Macao, Russia, and Iran. Still, the gap is smaller using PPP adjustments than using nominal rates. The remainder of this report will rely largely on market exchange rates because there are fewer data quality problems and they give a better indication of the ability to purchase on the international market, but the reader should keep in mind that such economic measures as GDP and defense spending will be larger for China, Russia, Iran, and North Korea when based on PPP rates than they are when based on market rates.

Future Projection: Narrower Income Gap but No Income Catch-Up

Two economic trends are likely to occur through 2030. First, the overall share of the global economy accounted for by the United States and its alliance partners is likely to continue falling. To the extent that U.S. adversaries can support proportionately larger military budgets, those nations can narrow the gap in defense spending. Second, the level of development of U.S. challengers is likely to stay well below that of the United States. To the extent that development (as measured by per capita GDP) influences military power, the United States and its alliance partners should stay ahead of their challengers.

This chapter has focused on nominal GDP to calculate shares of the world economy. Generally speaking, nominal GDP is the best indicator for the value of goods and services that a country can buy on global markets and the value of investments that can be made globally at any one time, and so it gives one indication of international economic power.[19] However, projecting nominal GDPs is fraught with

[19] Other options for projections are real GDP growth or growth of GDP in terms of PPP. None of these are the perfect indicator. Real growth shows the growth in quantity of output, and growth of GDP in terms of PPP is best used to show changes in the standard of living.

error because such projections, especially in dollar terms, must take account of real growth (the changes in *quantities* of goods and services produced), inflation (the changes in the *prices* of those goods and services in local currency), and exchange rates (how the output of one country is *valued* in terms of U.S. dollars).

We present some speculative projections to illustrate how shares of the global economy might look in 2030, based on specific modeling assumptions about nominal growth in each country (Table 3.1). Among the United States and its allies, U.S. nominal GDP grew at an annual rate of 4.5 percent from 1990 to 2017, and Japan grew at 1.6 percent. The U.S. Congressional Budget Office (CBO) projects annual nominal U.S. GDP

Table 3.1
Projected Nominal Growth Rates

Country or Country Group	Baseline (%)	Faster Challenger Growth (%)	Faster Allied Growth (%)
United States	4.1	4.1	4.5
NATO 28	2.0	2.0	3.3
Japan	1.5	1.5	1.6
Other Asia	3.8	3.8	6.1
China	9.0	13.2	9.0
Russia	3.0	4.3	3.0
Iran	2.0	4.2	2.0
Rest of world	5.0	5.0	5.0
World	4.4	5.1	4.9

SOURCE: Authors' scenarios based on data from World Bank, 2018.
NOTES: NATO 28 = 28 non-U.S. NATO members as of July 2018; "Other Asia" = U.S. treaty allies Australia, Korea, New Zealand, the Philippines, and Thailand; "China" = China, Hong Kong, and Macao because although the jurisdictions are currently under the one country–two systems model, it is likely that China would draw on Hong Kong and Macao as needed in wartime. The 2017 *National Security Strategy of the United States* identified China, Russia, Iran, and North Korea as challengers to the United States and its allies and to the global order (White House, 2017b). No GDP data were available for North Korea.

growth of 4.1 percent from 2017 through 2028.[20] Accordingly, we model U.S. future growth at 4.1 percent and Japanese as 1.5 percent (the latter to take account of demographic changes). By contrast, the NATO 28 (excluding the United States) grew at 3.3 percent, but these are aging societies and growth has slowed, so we project forward at 2.0 percent. And U.S. allies in Asia have grown at 6.1 percent but have also recently slowed; they are also heavily dependent on China, which we expect to slow, so we project the Asian allies forward at 3.8 percent. Among challengers, China's annual nominal growth rate was 13.2 percent from 1990 to 2017 and 10.3 percent from 2010 to 2017. Given that this has been fueled in part by unsustainable debt and that Chinese leadership is intent on slowing growth, however, we project forward at 9 percent. Russia's nominal GDP has been highly volatile and strongly related to oil and gas prices, and potentially low oil prices and continued sanctions can be expected to have a negative effect. The IMF suggests that unless there are significant reforms, Russia's economy will continue to struggle.[21] Accordingly, we project forward at 3.0 percent, below nominal growth of 2010 to 2017, a period that experienced both high oil prices (through 2014) and sanctions (starting in 2014). The outlook for Iran is also related to oil and gas prices and sanctions, but compared with Russia, Iran's internal problems are more severe, the nation has poorer economic management, and tougher sanctions have been instituted. Accordingly, we project forward at 2.0 percent. Finally, world nominal GDP growth averaged 4.8 percent from 1990 to 2017, but has averaged 2.9 percent since 2010. We project forward at 4.4 percent, meaning we project 5.0 percent growth for the parts of the world we have not included. We also provide alternate projections (the final two columns of Table 3.1) with further discussion later in this chapter.

In this scenario, the entire world economy grows from a nominal value of $80.7 trillion at market exchange rates in 2017 to $141.2 trillion in 2030; at a real growth rate of 2.8 percent, it grows from $80.0 trillion

---

[20] CBO, *The Budget and Economic Outlook: 2018 to 2028*, Washington, D.C., April 2018a.

[21] IMF, "Russian Federation: Staff Concluding Statement of the 2018 Article IV Mission," Washington, D.C., May 23, 2018a.

in 2010 dollars to $114.9 trillion.[22] China becomes the largest single-country economy in nominal terms at market rates in 2027, with 24.1 percent of world GDP, compared with 23.4 percent for the United States (Figure 3.3). By 2030, the GDP of NATO as a whole would be 40.2 percent of the global economy, and that of the United States and all its alliance partners would be 48.8 percent, still ahead of China and the other challengers, which collectively would account for 29.5 percent.

Figure 3.3
Projections for Share of Nominal World GDP Produced by the United States, Allies, and Challengers

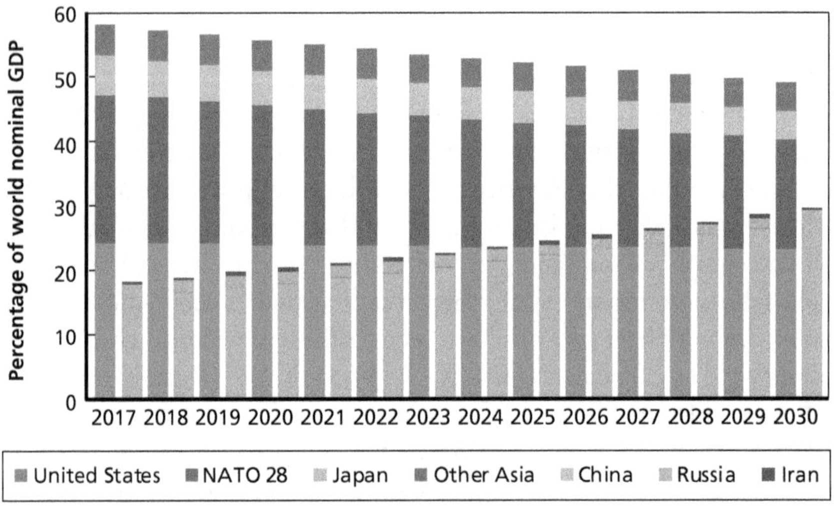

SOURCE: Authors' calculations based on data from World Bank, 2018.
NOTES: GDP is in terms of nominal U.S. dollars. "NATO 28" = 28 non-U.S. NATO members as of July 2018; "Other Asia" = U.S. treaty allies Australia, Korea, New Zealand, the Philippines, and Thailand; "China" = China, Hong Kong, and Macao because although the jurisdictions are currently under the one country–two systems model, it is likely that China would draw on Hong Kong and Macao as needed in wartime. The 2017 *National Security Strategy of the United States* identified China, Russia, Iran, and North Korea as challengers to the United States and its allies and to the global order (White House, 2017b). No GDP data were available for North Korea. See Table 3.1 for growth rates used in the projections.

---

[22] World GDP valued in constant 2010 dollars grew at an annual rate of 2.8 percent from 1990 to 2017 (World Bank, 2018).

We can vary these growth rates to see how the global share of income might change under different circumstances (Table 3.1). In the first variation, challengers grow more quickly. In the second, alliance members grow more quickly. In each case, we use the nominal growth rates from 1990 to 2017 as future growth rates for either challengers (variation one) or allies (variation two), and in each case, we hold rest of world growth at 5 percent, so that total world growth also varies in each scenario.

In the scenario where challengers grow faster than baseline, China would surpass the United States in terms of nominal GDP in 2023. By 2030, the United States and its NATO partners would account for 36.9 percent of global GDP, whereas China alone would account for 41.1 percent. The U.S. alliance as a whole would account for 44.8 percent; China, Russia, and Iran combined would account for 43.4 percent.

In the scenario where the U.S. alliance grows faster than baseline, China would surpass the United States in terms of nominal GDP in 2028. By 2030, the United States and its NATO partners would account for 41.8 percent of global GDP, whereas China would account for 25.8 percent. The U.S. alliance as a whole would account for 51.3 percent; China, Russia, and Iran combined would account for 27.7 percent.

An economy that is larger can, in turn, support larger, better-funded armed forces. But as already noted, the level of economic development is also important, especially in terms of equipment and personnel quality. The United States and its allies have a distinct advantage in this field because they are so far ahead of their challengers. We use real per capita GDP as a measure of development, and for simplicity, we compare the United States with China. In 2017, China's real per capita GDP in 2010 U.S. dollars was $7,300, compared with $53,100 for the United States. If both countries grew at their long-term annual growth rates (8.9 percent for China, 1.4 percent for the United States for the period 1990–2017), then their respective real per capita GDPs by 2030 would be $22,200 and $63,800, respectively—still an enormous difference. If, instead, they were to grow at their more recent rates (7.1 percent for China and 1.3 percent for the United States for the period 2010–2017), then these figures would be $17,700 and $63,200. It is likely that the United States will grow at something close to this latter rate. It is far less likely that China will continue to grow even at the high levels of its more recent pace.

Europe's levels of development and innovation potential also add to the capabilities of the U.S.-led alliance. It is well recognized that Europe's economic growth likely will be low through 2030, largely because of demographics. But it has high levels of innovation, and this is unlikely to decline through 2030.[23]

There is one important caveat to discerning the relationship between size of economy and funding of armed forces, alluded to at the beginning of this chapter. Personnel costs are generally lower in developing countries, so comparing defense budgets dollar-for-dollar provides an incomplete comparison. This might also extend to indigenously sourced equipment. Both of these factors have sparked tremendous debate about the actual size of the Chinese defense budget.[24]

One way to formally calculate this is with PPP exchange rates, discussed earlier, rather than market exchange rates. Personnel costs are an obvious candidate for conversion at PPP rates, but other equipment and costs could be as well. Especially for China, given the opacity of its defense budget, it is difficult to determine which costs are best translated at PPP rates, so we provide a range of estimates. At market rates, the U.S. defense budget was $606 billion in 2017 and the Chinese defense budget was $228 billion. If 10 percent of the Chinese defense budget were converted at PPP rates, that budget would be equivalent to $249 billion. If 50 percent of the defense budget were converted at PPP rates, the equivalent would be $331 billion; at 90 percent, the equivalent would be $414 billion.[25] These are all well below

---

23 These observations stem from interviews with government officials and researchers in London and Brussels in April 2018.

24 Sydney J. Freedberg, Jr., "US Defense Budget Not That Much Bigger Than China, Russia: Gen. Milley," *Breaking Defense*, May 22, 2018.

25 In 2017, the ratio of China's nominal PPP GDP to its market-rate GDP was 1.9; in terms of standard of living, this means China was actually 1.9 times richer, and a dollar would go 1.9 times further, than market rates would imply. Thus, to calculate these adjusted defense

the size of the U.S. budget, but they draw closer to equivalency as more costs are completely indigenously sourced.

PPP conversion is actually a countervailing force on an increasing Chinese defense budget over the longer term. As a country develops, its PPP rates converge to the market rate. The conversion factor was 1.9 in 2017 but likely will be lower in 2030. This means that the basic story already described will still hold—under most scenarios, the economies and defense budgets of U.S. challengers will be less than those of the United States and its alliance partners.

Implications for the U.S. Air Force and the Future of Warfare

The United States and its allies gain numerous advantages from their dominance in the global economy. As the largest trading economies, they can set global technological, environmental, and other standards for internationally traded goods and services. With strong, market-oriented financial and innovation systems and high levels of education, they can more easily support technological advances.

Having a larger economy also supports actions more directly related to war. First, larger economies can afford to stay ahead of their rivals in quality, quantity, and technology of military equipment. This pertains directly to equipment and weapons used by USAF. Second, economic sanctions, instituted as an adjunct to or in lieu of military activity, will be more effective based on the size of the economy instituting them. We consider these two economic trends in Chapters Six and Seven.

---

budgets, we multiplied the indigenously sourced portion by 1.9. As noted in the text, it is difficult to assess exactly how much of the defense budget should be converted at PPP rates.

CHAPTER FOUR

Trend 3: The Rise of China

One of the most important events in the post–World War II era has been the rise of China as an economic power. In 1960, China's GDP constituted 4.4 percent of world nominal GDP at market exchange rates. Over the next two decades, failed economic policies in China and better economic policies abroad shrank China's GDP to 1.7 percent of the world total. But starting in the late 1970s, China's economy started to grow thanks to internal economic reform and China opening up to world trade and investment. By 2016, China's economy constituted 14.8 percent of the world total when measured at nominal market exchange rates, was the second-largest in the world, and was second in international trade, behind only the United States.[1]

With this increase in economic might has come increased defense spending, increased involvement in international security affairs, and increased interest in playing a more prominent role in international institutions or starting parallel institutions. In 2015, China lobbied for its currency, the renminbi (RMB), to be included in the IMF unit of account, called the special drawing right (SDR), which is a basket of currencies that meet certain criteria. The IMF did so in 2016, although many international economists questioned whether the RMB actually

[1] World Bank, 2018. On the basis of PPP, the Chinese economy was larger than that of the United States. In 2017, China's GDP was $12.2 trillion in market terms and $23.3 billion in PPP terms. That same year, U.S. GDP was $19.4 trillion in market and PPP terms. For assessing standard of living, per capita GDP in PPP terms is a good measure. In 2017, China's per capita GDP was $8,800 in market terms and $16,800 in PPP terms. U.S. per capita GDP was $59,500 by both measures.

met the criteria.[2] Likewise, in 2016, a new development bank called the Asian Infrastructure Investment Bank opened with 57 founding members, led by China.[3] The United States opposed the bank and encouraged its allies not to join, but in the end, the United Kingdom, France, Italy, and Germany—all G7 leading economies—were all founding members, and Canada has since joined.[4]

The rise of China has led the U.S. government to view China more critically, and recent U.S. policy guidance has been designed to shape China's rise in directions more agreeable to the United States. By late 2017, the United States had identified China as a revisionist power and competitor that is stealing U.S. intellectual property and technology, as a country that is trying to "erode American security and prosperity," as a country that wants "to shape a world antithetical to U.S. values and interests," and as a country wishing to reorder the Indo-Pacific region in its favor.[5]

---

[2] Edwin M. Truman, "The Chinese Renminbi Is Not a Freely Usable Currency Yet," Washington, D.C.: Peterson Institute for International Economics, August 7, 2015; IMF, "IMF Launches New SDR Basket Including Chinese Renminbi, Determines New Currency Amounts," press release, September 30, 2016.

[3] "Backgrounder: The AIIB," Xinhua, January 16, 2016.

[4] The United States has sole veto power at the World Bank and dominates the Asian Development Bank jointly with Japan. Although the U.S. government did not publicly specify its opposition to the Asian Infrastructure Investment Bank, it reportedly expressed concerns that the new China-dominated bank would have lax governance standards, especially regarding the environment and anti-corruption (Thomas Wright, "A Special Argument: The U.S., the U.K., and the AIIB," The Brookings Institution, March 13, 2015). The Asian Infrastructure Investment Bank was viewed as a competitor to the Asian Development Bank. Since its founding, it has partnered with most major development banks (Asian Infrastructure Investment Bank, "Partnerships," webpage, 2018). As of late 2018, assessments of its operations have generally been positive (see Sara Hsu, "How China's Asian Infrastructure Investment Bank Fared Its First Year," *Forbes*, January 14, 2017; and Tamar Gutner, "AIIB: Is the Chinese-Led Development Bank a Role Model?" Council on Foreign Relations, blog post, June 25, 2018).

[5] White House, 2017b. China is identified as a revisionist power (p. 25), as a competitor stealing intellectual property and technology (p. 21), as a country trying to erode American security and prosperity (p. 2), and as a country trying to reshape the world and reorder the Indo-Pacific (p. 25).

The rise of China raises three broad issues related to economic trends and war. The first is how China will participate in or shape the current international system—whether it will substantially uphold the current system, or instead change the system in ways to benefit itself to the detriment of the United States and its partners and allies. The second is whether and how the economic expansion of China—for example, through its Belt and Road Initiative (BRI)—will lead to military expansion. The third is the health of the Chinese economy itself, whether a slowdown or crisis will lead to increased nationalism by the government and perhaps aggressive actions against neighbors and U.S. allies.

Context: Policy Changes a Cause for Concern

China's growth among major economies has been unprecedented. From 1960 to 2017, its aggregate real GDP grew 9.7 percent annually, the second-fastest among all countries (behind only Equatorial Guinea), and its per capita GDP grew 8.9 percent annually.[6]

This growth, by itself, does not support the drawing of specific conclusions about future wars. War involving China and other great powers is always possible, but a recent RAND report has assessed the probability as low, albeit with increasing uncertainty.[7] The report identified several potential flashpoints, such as the South China Sea, Taiwan, and the cyber domain (such as an attack by one country on the networks of another). That report viewed economic issues as an outcome—economic damage to both sides—rather than as a cause, with any conflict spreading into the economic and space realms.

Likewise, some research has viewed the overall threat to the international system as low. China has been a participant in international institutions and to date there has been little evidence that it is trying to

---

6 World Bank, 2018.

7 James Dobbins, Andrew Scobell, Edmund J. Burke, David C. Gompert, Derek Grossman, Eric Heginbotham, and Howard J. Shatz, *Conflict with China Revisited: Prospects, Consequences, and Strategies for Deterrence*, Santa Monica, Calif.: RAND Corporation, PE-248-A, 2017.

undermine them. Indeed, there is a sense that China will not damage such institutions because they provide greater legitimacy.[8] Overall, China can be viewed as a conditional supporter of the international order and its institutions that harbors a desire for more influence in exchange for its support.[9] Although actively participating in such institutions, it has also established parallel institutions, the most prominent example being the Asian Infrastructure Investment Bank.

However, the historical record suggests that recent developments in China's policies might heighten risks of conflict. The worry is not so much China's growth. The United States grew rapidly and surpassed Great Britain as the world's leading economy without any conflict between the two countries. In fact, U.S. involvement in World War I and then the firm alliance between the two countries in World War II created the conditions for what as of 2018 has been two centuries of Anglo-U.S. rule-setting for the global economy. Rather, it is the nature of changes in China's economic policies that creates concern.[10] Although China is a far

---

[8] This observation stems from interviews with government officials and researchers in London, Brussels, Berlin, and Warsaw in April 2018.

[9] For a comprehensive assessment of China and the international order, see Michael J. Mazarr, Timothy R. Heath, and Astrid Stuth Cevallos, *China and the International Order*, Santa Monica, Calif.: RAND Corporation, RR-2423-OSD, 2018.

[10] This is a different argument than that raised by Graham Allison recently (Graham Allison, "The Thucydides Trap: Are the U.S. and China Headed for War?" *The Atlantic*, September 24, 2015; Graham Allison, *Destined for War? Can America and China Escape Thucydides's Trap?* New York, Houghton Mifflin Harcourt Publishing Company, 2017a; Graham Allison, "War Between China and the United States Isn't Inevitable, but It's Likely: An Excerpt from Graham Allison's *Destined for War*," *National Post*, March 5, 2018). Allison defined the Thucydides trap as war that occurs when one great power rises to disrupt the position of a dominant state; he wrote that war need not always occur, but often does (Graham Allison, "How Trump and Xi Could Stumble Into War," *Washington Post*, March 31, 2017b). He argues that a rising power's growing entitlement and sense of importance combined with the leading power's desire to defend the status quo could lead to war. In contrast, our argument is that clashing economic systems that result in the erosion of economic opportunities could raise the possibility of war, regardless of whether powers are rising or leading. In fact, one critique of the Thucydides trap argument is that it either neglects causation or gets the causation wrong (James C. MacDougall, "Review Essay: Destined for War: Can America and China Escape Thucydides's Trap?" *Parameters*, Vol. 47, No. 2, Summer 2017; Declan Sullivan, "Destined for Competition: An Analysis of Graham Allison's Thucydides Trap," *The Strategy Bridge*, January 24, 2018).

more open economy in the 21st century than it was through the second half of the 20th century, knowledgeable observers have noted an increase of government intervention in the economy and state control under Xi Jinping. It is too early to say whether this is a longer-term trend or only a slight reversal.[11] An analysis of economic trends and war dating from just before the start of World War II found that greater state control of an economy acts as an impetus to war, as do rising trade barriers.[12] Likewise, a more recent analysis has found that armed conflict becomes more likely as protectionism and state involvement in an economy rises.[13]

China remains a highly protectionist economy and appears to be increasing state intervention in the economy. And the rise of China is the first time in well over 100 years that a protectionist, state-controlled economy has played a prominent role in global economic exchange and governance. Thus, the historical record indicates these changes are a valid cause for concern, but it is too weak a signal to govern policy.

Historical Trend: Rapid Integration, Increasing Vulnerability

China has rapidly integrated into the international economy and international institutions. Given the evidence we have presented about trade and war, this alone served to lower the risk of conflict. At the same time, the Chinese economy has become more vulnerable to internal disruptions. In this section, we review these issues, focusing on the period since 2000.

---

[11] Christopher Balding, "China Bets on More State Control for 2018," Bloomberg, December 26, 2017b; Barry Naughton, "Economic Policy in the Aftermath of the 19th Party Congress," *China Leadership Monitor*, No. 55, January 23, 2018. In its most recent Article IV report on China, the IMF noted that "continued widespread, and from some perspectives increasing, state intervention threatens the goal of high-quality growth" (IMF, *People's Republic of China: 2018 Article IV Consultation*, press release; staff report; staff statement and statement by the Executive Director for the People's Republic of China, IMF Country Report No. 18/240, July 2018b.

[12] Robbins, 1968.

[13] Morelli and Sonno, 2017.

The prime example of integration into international institutions is the accession of China to the WTO on December 11, 2001, more than 15 years after it initially applied to join the GATT.[14] At the time, the accession was seen as extremely positive. China was then the largest trading nation outside the WTO. The accession agreement included market-access commitments and other promises that exceeded those usually made by countries applying for membership.[15] In addition, accession was seen as having served the purpose of empowering reformers who wanted a more open China, and the general consensus was that accession would add stability to the U.S.-China relationship.[16]

Now that China has been in the WTO for more than 15 years, assessments are more mixed. In January 2018, the U.S. Trade Representative issued a report saying that China has not opened as U.S. policymakers had hoped, and that "it seems clear that the United States erred in supporting China's entry into the WTO on terms that have proven to be ineffective in securing China's embrace of an open, market-oriented trade regime."[17] Notably, this is not an argument that China should not have been in the WTO; rather, it is an argument about the terms of that accession.

In fact, those supporting China's inclusion in the WTO note that the world and the United States are better off with China in than out and that dispute resolution has worked.[18] Examples of this are the fact that the United States did not have to make any liberalizing changes to its trade policy, but China had to drop tariffs on many items, open up

---

14 World Trade Organization, "China," webpage, undated-a.

15 These included commitments to liberalizing a variety of domestic economic activities that previously had been off-limits in international negotiations, such as aspects of financial services, telecommunications, agriculture, and intellectual property. Nicholas R. Lardy, "Issues in China's WTO Accession," Washington, D.C., Brookings Institution, testimony, May 9, 2001.

16 Joseph Fewsmith, "China and the WTO: The Politics Behind the Agreement," National Bureau of Asian Research, November 1999.

17 U.S. Trade Representative, *2017 Report to Congress on China's WTO Compliance*, Washington, D.C., January 2018a, p. 2.

18 Simon Lester, "Why China's Entry into the WTO Has Been Good for the U.S.," *MarketWatch*, January 23, 2018.

to agricultural trade, and allow foreign service providers to operate in China. The one agreement the United States had to make was to offer China permanent most-favored-nation status, meaning it had to treat China no worse than any other WTO member; in fact, the United States had been applying this standard since 1980.[19] What is generally agreed upon is that the WTO by itself cannot be used to address many of the challenges that China raises.

The WTO is not the only institution in which China has expanded its influence. The chief economist of the World Bank has traditionally been an American. In 2008, Justin Yifu Lin, then a professor and founding director of the China Centre for Economic Research at Peking University, became the bank's first non-U.S. chief economist. After he started his World Bank position, even greater changes occurred. In 2010, the World Bank and the IMF both introduced major reforms in their voting structure to give developing countries a greater voice in their governance.[20] As the largest developing country, China benefited. These changes took effect in 2016, after U.S. congressional approval in 2015, although the United States remained the only single country with veto rights. More changes occurred in 2018, when World Bank members agreed to a capital increase that also involved raising China's voting share from 4.45 percent to 5.71 percent, placing it third behind Japan and the United States, but still leaving the United States with a veto.[21]

At the same time, China has been developing its own institutions, both formal and informal. The most notable is the Asian Infrastructure Investment Bank, as noted. But others exist as well, such as the Forum on China-Africa Cooperation and the China-CELAC Forum, in which China meets with the Community of Latin American and Caribbean States.

---

[19] Philip Levy, "Was Letting China into the WTO a Mistake?" *Foreign Affairs*, April 2, 2018.

[20] Sameer Vasta, "World Bank Gets Capital Increase and Reforms Voting Power," *Voices*, World Bank Blog, April 25, 2010; IMF, "IMF Executive Board Approves Major Overhaul of Quotas and Governance," Washington, D.C., Press Release No. 10/418, November 5, 2010.

[21] Josh Zumbrun, "How China and the U.S. Both Come Out Winners in Boost to World Bank," *Wall Street Journal*, April 23, 2018.

The most ambitious venture to reshape the world, however, is not so much an institution as a vision: the BRI. Under the umbrella of the BRI, China intends to create new land and sea corridors and other types of connectivity linking East, Southeast, and Central Asia with the Middle East and Africa all the way through to Western Europe.[22] Specifically, China envisions the BRI to have five types of connectivity:

1. policy coordination
2. transport and other infrastructure facilities, including adoption of common technical standards
3. unimpeded trade, focusing on the removal of investment and trade barriers and the creation of sound business environments
4. financial integration
5. people-to-people bonds.[23]

The BRI is on its way to becoming the central organizing principle for China and for much of the world. Including itself, China reports that the BRI covers more than 70 countries. These countries contain almost two-thirds of the world's population and about one-third of its nominal GDP; without China, these figures would be 19 percent of world GDP and 47 percent of its population, indicating that many of these countries are quite poor.[24] Branded with the Belt and Road label, numerous railway routes from China to Europe have

---

[22] The proposal was expanded upon in two subsequent documents: National Development and Reform Commission, *Vision and Actions on Jointly Building Silk Road Economic Belt and 21st-Century Maritime Silk Road*, Beijing: Ministry of Foreign Affairs, Ministry of Commerce of the People's Republic of China, with State Council Authorization, March 28, 2015; and China Institute of International Studies, *China's Diplomatic Efforts to Promote Energy and Resources Cooperation Along the "One Belt and One Road,"* Beijing, CIIS Report No. 5, May 2015.

[23] National Development and Reform Commission, 2015.

[24] In a May 2018 publication, China counted 71 countries in addition to itself as being part of Belt and Road (Cheng Xiaobo, ed. [程晓波主编], *Big Data Report on Trade Cooperation Under the Belt and Road Initiative* [一带一路贸易合作大数据报告], Belt and Road Big Data Center of the State Information Center [国家信息中心"一带一路"大数据中心] and SINOIMEX [大连瀚闻资讯有限公司], May 2018, p. IX).

already opened, including routes to Hamburg, Duisberg, and Leipzig in Germany; London; and Madrid.

Despite its rapid growth, its role as a major trading power, and the vision it is setting for the world, China has numerous vulnerabilities as well. One feature of the Chinese economy is that it is unusually unbalanced; it invests too much and consumes too little. Its levels of investment as a share of GDP far exceed those of other rapidly growing East Asian economies, even when those countries were at China's level of development.[25] This has resulted in overinvestment, which is inefficient for the economy and signals poorer growth prospects ahead.

Much of this investment and related growth has been fueled by debt, and there are fears that this debt growth is unsustainable, raising risks of economic problems. The problem has reached such a magnitude that in August 2017, the IMF warned that China's credit growth could be on a dangerous trajectory and said that excessive credit growth had bought China at least a percentage point worth of annual growth over the preceding five years.[26] Others argue that growth has actually been much lower, suggesting that if unproductive debt were properly accounted for, actual annual growth would be below 3 percent.[27]

Regardless of actual growth, China's leaders have recognized that they need to rebalance the economy from export- and investment-led growth to consumption- and innovation-led growth. Various plans and policy statements have been issued. For example, at the Nineteenth Party Congress, then–Communist Party Secretary Xi praised the implementation of China's new innovation-driven development strategy and supply-side structural reform, and he called for more progress not only in innovation-driven development but in improving "systems and mechanisms for stimulating consumer spending, and

---

[25] David Dollar, *China's Rebalancing: Lessons from East Asian Economic History*, Washington, D.C.: Brookings Institution, John L. Thornton China Center Working Paper Series, October 2013.

[26] Joong Shik Kang, Sally Chen, and Daniel Law, "Credit Booms—Is China Different?" in International Monetary Fund, *People's Republic of China: Selected Issues*, Washington, D.C., IMF Country Report No. 17/248, August 2017.

[27] Michael Pettis, "China's Growth Miracle Has Run Out of Steam," *Financial Times*, November 19, 2017.

leverage the fundamental role of consumption in promoting economic growth."[28] Although Xi called for markets to play "the decisive role in resource allocation," he also called for party leadership in all aspects of society, for upholding and improving "China's basic socialist economic system and socialist distribution system," and for "state capital in becoming stronger, doing better, and growing bigger."[29]

Certainly, reforms have taken place. But observers see little being done to truly reform China's system in the direction that independent analysts, state researchers, and even top policymakers have called for. Even if these reforms take place, China has a long way to go. Despite economic development that has lifted hundreds of millions of people out of poverty, it still has hundreds of millions of people in poverty. With low levels of education, poor nutrition, and poor health, it is unlikely that much of its population will ever contribute to the type of consumption- and innovation-led growth that China is aiming for.[30]

Future Projection: More Global, Yet More Closed Off

Three aspects of China's future will play a role in the relationship between the Chinese economy and war. The first is the trajectory of China's growth and the role it will play in international institutions. The second, which is related, is the evolution of the BRI. The third, also related, is China's internal economic health.

The first two of these are important for the openness of the global economy. If countries lose trading opportunities (and thus also lose opportunities for growth and development), then a risk of conflict could rise, however small that increase might be. Should China itself run into economic problems, domestic unrest could challenge the gov-

---

28 Xi Jinping, "Secure a Decisive Victory in Building a Moderately Prosperous Society in All Respects and Strive for the Great Success of Socialism with Chinese Characteristics for a New Era," full text of Xi Jinping's report at the 19th CPC National Congress, delivered at the 19th National Congress of the Communist Party of China, October 18, 2017.

29 Xi, 2017.

30 Andrew Browne, "The Underclass That Threatens Xi's 'China Dream,'" *Wall Street Journal*, December 5, 2017.

ernment and rule of the Communist Party of China—which could, in turn, engage in a more adventurous foreign policy of rallying nationalism to retain support instead of relying on economic growth for that cause.

China is at once reaching out to the world and closing off. It is becoming more involved in international institutions and multilateral action, with greater voting power in the IMF and World Bank and with its own institutions, such as the Asian Infrastructure Investment Bank. At the same time, there are troubling indications that it is becoming more closed, suggesting that if it proves decisive in setting global rules, trading opportunities could decline. A prime example is the Made in China 2025 plan, released in 2015, to be followed by two more such plans, to "transform China into a leading manufacturing power by the year 2049," the 100th anniversary of the founding of the People's Republic of China.[31] The plan focuses on ten sectors, specifically "new information technology, numerical control tools and robotics, aerospace equipment, ocean engineering equipment and high-tech ships, railway equipment, energy saving and new energy vehicles, power equipment, new materials, biological medicine and medical devices, and agricultural machinery."[32] To achieve its goals, it defines nine tasks, such as "strengthening the industrial base" and "fostering Chinese brands"; implementation is intended to be "market-oriented, though guided by the government."[33]

Many governments around the world develop plans to foster economic growth or spur innovation and technological development, but business groups in the United States and Europe have viewed Made in China as an attempt to unfairly take global leadership in advanced industries.[34] An analysis by a China-oriented research organization found that the plan would systematically benefit domestic producers

---

[31] "'Made in China 2025' Plan Unveiled," Xinhua, May 19, 2015.

[32] "'Made in China 2025' Plan Unveiled," 2015.

[33] "'Made in China 2025' Plan Unveiled," 2015.

[34] See, for example, European Chamber, *China Manufacturing 2025: Putting Industrial Policy Ahead of Market Forces*, Beijing, 2017; and U.S. Chamber of Commerce, *Made in China 2025: Global Ambitions Built on Local Protections*, Washington, D.C., 2017.

and disadvantage foreign businesses.[35] Although multilateral institutions have not evaluated the plan, the World Bank's China country director has noted that the plan is one aspect of more active industrial policy, which had been less emphasized following the reforms started in 1978.[36] U.S. trade actions in the spring and summer of 2018 were designed to directly counter the Made in China effort.[37]

In addition, there are concerns that the BRI will not open opportunities but will instead create significant barriers to world trade and to economies that are not in the BRI orbit. Some of these concerns are expressed by nations that might be economically disadvantaged even by fair competition from China, and some claims are unproved. Nonetheless, they are motivating policy. There are three broad economic concerns with the BRI. The first is that many of its projects will not prove economically viable, leaving someone—China, a borrowing Chinese company, a borrowing foreign company, or a borrowing foreign government—with debts that cannot be paid.[38] Such debts, if they are sovereign, could lead to budget challenges and balance of payments difficulties in Belt and Road partner countries.[39] They could also lead to China exercising greater political and diplomatic leverage over these countries. Second, as China becomes more active in Belt and Road countries, it could also be setting global regulatory and technical standards that could provide advantages to Chinese companies over all others.[40] The final concern, voiced by all but one of the EU

[35] Jost Wübbeke, Mirjam Meissner, Max J. Zenglein, Jaqueline Ives, and Björn Conrad, *Made in China 2025: The Making of a High-Tech Superpower and Consequences for Industrial Countries*, Berlin: Mercator Institute for China Studies, MERICS Papers on China No. 2, December 2016.

[36] Bert Hofman, "Reflections on Forty Years of China's Reforms," speech at the Fudan University's Fanhai School of International Finance, January 2018.

[37] U.S. Trade Representative, "USTR Issues Tariffs on Chinese Products in Response to Unfair Trade Practices," Press Release, Washington, D.C., June 15, 2018b.

[38] Fitch Ratings, "China's One Belt, One Road Initiative Brings Risks," press release, January 25, 2017.

[39] Christine Lagarde, "Belt and Road Initiative: Strategies to Deliver in the Next Phase," Beijing, speech at IMF-PBC Conference, April 12, 2018.

[40] Andrew Polk, "China Is Quietly Setting Global Standards," Bloomberg, May 6, 2018.

ambassadors in Beijing, is that the entire effort could end up hampering free trade, thereby changing the global trading order.[41] Although the EU document was not released, it reportedly dealt with such issues as preferential treatment for Chinese firms for public procurement in Belt and Road projects, transparency in public procurement, and the enforcement of environmental and social standards.[42]

For now, U.S. partners and allies are conflicted. They believe they can benefit economically from trade and investment with China. They also believe that, in contrast to their growing perceptions of the United States, China is an ally in upholding international institutions and a constructive partner in those institutions. In their view, as long as China benefits from those institutions, it will be a supporter. To Europe, especially, this is important.[43]

While these nations view China as an institutional ally, they also view it as an increasingly unfair competitor, much as the United States does. Among the issues are lack of equal treatment in public procurement; insufficient reciprocity; constrained market access for EU investors; and the environmental, social, and technical standards to which Chinese firms adhere internationally. But the EU wants to maintain the global institutional system, even without the United States. The formulation is that, given the rhetoric and policies of the United States as of early 2018, the EU is aligned with the United States on commercial interests (meaning such issues as market access and transparency in government procurement) but not systemic interests (meaning such issues as support for the WTO and its various efforts to enforce trade

---

[41] Dana Heide, Till Hoppe, Stephan Scheuer, and Klaus Stratmann, "EU Ambassadors Band Together Against Silk Road," Handelsblatt Global, April 17, 2018. The ambassador from Hungary did not sign.

[42] Heide et al., 2018.

[43] These observations stem from interviews with government officials and researchers in London, Brussels, Berlin, and Warsaw in April 2018. Note that not all European officials view China this way. Some said that China, in league with Russia, was trying to undermine the international system, while others noted their opinion was that China was using the system without accepting it.

rules), whereas the EU is aligned with China on systemic issues but not commercial ones, given China's rhetoric and policies as of early 2018.[44]

Beyond China's stance toward the global economy, there is the issue of its internal economic stability. Countries rarely, if ever, have growth over the long term without significant setbacks. China has not had a major economic crisis in decades, and it is not clear how well leaders will handle one. The government's response to a stock market crash in 2015 did not breed international investor confidence in China's ability to handle unusual economic events.[45]

Just as China's reaction to economic crises is uncertain, its innovation potential is also uncertain. Although it is now being portrayed as an innovation leader, it has been an innovation follower for all of its previous development.[46] China's leaders have reportedly been concerned that growth could plateau with China still a middle-income country, leading to stagnation not just in growth but job creation.[47]

In some ways, Chinese growth raises concerns (especially regarding China's stance toward the global economy), and lack of growth also raises concerns (regarding how Chinese society and the Communist Party will react to that trend). Therefore, through 2030, the key uncertainties will be how well China maintains its growth, how much support it lends to the institutional foundations of an open world economy, and how open it remains. Significant backsliding on any of these issues could lead to greater international tensions.

---

[44] These observations stem from interviews with government officials and researchers in London, Brussels, Berlin, and Warsaw in April 2018. Notably, as of 2019, this may be changing. In March 2019, a European Commission document noted that in different policy areas, China was a cooperation partner, a negotiating partner, an economic competitor, and "a systemic rival promoting alternative models of governance." See European Commission, *EU-China—A Strategic Outlook*, Joint Communication to the European Parliament, the European Council and the Council, Strasbourg: JOIN(2019) 5 final, March 12, 2019.

[45] Nargiza Salidjanova, "China's Stock Market Collapse and Government's Response," Issue Brief, U.S.-China Economic and Security Review Commission, July 13, 2015.

[46] These observations stem from interviews with government officials and researchers in London, Brussels, Berlin, and Warsaw in April 2018.

[47] Zhang Zhengfu, Liu Jie, and Wang Xiuqiong, "China Focus: How China Can Avoid the Middle Income Trap in a New Era," *Xinhua*, October 23, 2017.

Implications for the U.S. Air Force and the Future of Warfare

The rise of China has various implications for the future of warfare. A direct effect, as we noted in the chapter on relative economic size in the world, is a greater ability to fund its armed forces.[48] There are several less direct effects that heighten risk.[49]

First among them is the extent to which Chinese security interests will follow Chinese economic interests. As of early 2018, China had only one overseas military base, in Djibouti, inaugurated in July 2017 and signaling its desire to protect its growing economic interests in Africa.[50] Notably, the highest-grossing Chinese film features a former Chinese special operations soldier rescuing Chinese civilians in Africa.[51] If Chinese military bases expand, they will get closer not only to

---

[48] Implications of China's technological development in the defense industry and the potential for U.S. overmatch of opposing forces can be found in another report in this series, Morgan and Cohen, 2020.

[49] China has historically run trade surpluses with the United States, and as a consequence has amassed $1.1 trillion worth of Treasury securities, the largest holding of all foreign purchasers as of October 2018, and 18.4 percent of all foreign holdings (U.S. Department of the Treasury, "Major Foreign Holders of Treasury Securities," online data, December 17, 2018). Note also that as of October 2018, total Treasury securities net of premium and discount, including intragovernmental holdings, amounted to $21.6 trillion (with China holding 5.3 percent), and Treasury securities held only by the public amounted to $15.8 trillion, with China holding 7.2 percent (U.S. Department of the Treasury, *Monthly Treasury Statement: Receipts and Outlays of the United States Government for Fiscal Year 2019 Through October 31, 2018, and Other Periods*, Washington, D.C.: Bureau of the Fiscal Service, 2018). There has been speculation that China could use the sale of these securities as a point of leverage over the United States, causing ill effects on the U.S. economy. However, doing so would be difficult and could cause ill effects on the Chinese economy as well (see, for example, "Is It a Risk for America That China Holds over $1 Trillion in U.S. Debt?" China Power, February 2, 2016; and Brad W. Setser, "What Would Happen If China Started Selling Off Its Treasury Portfolio?" Washington, D.C., Council on Foreign Relations, June 21, 2018).

[50] John Fei, "China's Overseas Military Base in Djibouti: Features, Motivations, and Policy Implications," *China Brief*, Vol. 17, Issue 17, December 22, 2017.

[51] Patrick Frater, "'Wolf Warrior II's' Massive Success Forces Studios to Rethink China Approach," *Variety*, August 31, 2017.

U.S. military installations but also to those of U.S. allies and Chinese rivals that the United States might support. China's economic expansion has occurred largely in concentric circles, giving priority to nearby Southeast Asia and Central Asia, then to the Middle East, and then Africa and Latin America. If the armed forces were to follow the same pattern, frictions could develop or become magnified in Southeast and South Asia.

China has also been investing in ports worldwide. One estimate held that in just the period between June 2016 and June 2017, China had announced plans to buy or invest in nine overseas ports for a total of $20.1 billion, more than double the amount of the year before.[52] Many of these investments likely will provide much-needed capital and improvements to these ports. Some, however, could serve a dual role as locations for China's military forces. For example, in late 2017, Sri Lanka gave China the port of Hambantota and 15,000 acres of land around it because of what had become unpayable debts. The port is on a critical military waterway near India, and although the lease forbids military activity, that can be changed by the government of Sri Lanka.[53] One analysis found that China's port investment in the Indo-Pacific has a goal of expanding China's military presence and that unofficial discussion in China notes national security interests and the goal of building dual-use infrastructure for use by China's navy.[54]

A related phenomenon is whether growing Chinese centrality in the global economy will encourage countries to lessen their security relationships with the United States and enhance them with China. Separate research at RAND discusses potential U.S. economic responses to China's BRI.[55] In the security realm, if countries perceive

---

[52] James Kynge, "China Purchases of Overseas Ports Top $20bn in Past Year," *Financial Times*, July 16, 2017.

[53] Maria Abi-Habib, "How China Got Sri Lanka to Cough Up a Port," *New York Times*, June 25, 2018.

[54] Devin Thorne and Ben Spevack, *Harbored Ambitions: How China's Port Investments Are Strategically Reshaping the Indo-Pacific*, Washington, D.C., C4ADS, April 2018.

[55] James Dobbins, Howard J. Shatz, and Suhail Ali Wyne, *Russia Is a Rogue, Not a Peer; China Is a Peer, Not a Rogue: Different Challenges, Different Responses*, Santa Monica, Calif.:

that China is important to their economic stability and well-being, and if they perceive China as a largely benign security provider, they might be more willing to welcome Chinese security cooperation or bases, or at least tolerate a Chinese security presence on their borders. This could weaken U.S. security relationships and lessen U.S. ability to respond to challenges.

Accordingly, DoD and USAF should stress their ability to partner reliably with nations in Southeast Asia, Central Asia, and Africa. Expansion of USAF foreign military training, invitation to military schools, increasing the number and quality of air attachés, and other programs can demonstrate that the United States is the premier power with which those nations should engage, in spite of the recent overtures from China.

The final implication is the unpredictable nature of China's response to economic stagnation. Debt has powered China's GDP growth.[56] Although the extent of this is debated, it is largely agreed that debt accumulation cannot continue, but whether it will result in slower growth or some kind of crisis is unknown.[57] In either case, a basic compact between the Communist Party of China and the people of China—that the party gains some degree of legitimacy from the economic gains over which it has presided—will have been damaged.

There is great uncertainty because in the post-reform era, China has not dealt with a sustained slowdown or deep economic crisis that it could not solve with more debt. The question is what the government's response might be. One response could be enhanced nationalism. Even as early as 1989, the party was enhancing its legitimacy through appeals to nationalism.[58] This nationalism could become a political force beyond party control. It is also possible that party leaders could

---

RAND Corporation, PE-310-A, 2019.

[56] Pettis, 2017.

[57] Michael Pettis, "China Was Never Likely to Have a Debt Crisis," CNBC, February 28, 2018; Jake van der Kamp, "My Prediction: The Coming Collapse of China's Ponzi Scheme Economy," *South China Morning Post*, August 27, 2017.

[58] Minxin Pei, "US-China Conflict Risks New Cold War," *Nikkei Asian Review*, January 24, 2018.

retain control by enhancing that nationalism with aggressive action beyond China's borders or by harnessing nationalism to enhance societal cohesion in overcoming economic difficulties. There is no way to predict which path will be chosen; planning should account for all of them.

In all these cases, war risks would likely be higher closer to China. China prioritizes security in regions closest to its borders, which is where the most-difficult security challenges are, including disputes over the South China Sea and fears of terrorist influences near its western borders.[59] But as China's security interests spread, so does the potential for Chinese military action farther abroad. In China's international economic relations, factors to watch include the most-active locations of Chinese economic involvement abroad, lending to specific countries, and greater security involvement abroad. In China's domestic economy, factors to watch include debt sustainability, job creation and destruction, and official actions regarding economic disruptions.

---

[59] Andrew Scobell, Bonny Lin, Howard J. Shatz, Michael Johnson, Larry Hanauer, Michael S. Chase, Astrid Stuth Cevallos, Ivan W. Rasmussen, Arthur Chan, Aaron Strong, Eric Warner, and Logan Ma, *At the Dawn of Belt and Road: China in the Developing World*, Santa Monica, Calif.: RAND Corporation, RR-2273-A, 2018.

CHAPTER FIVE

Trend 4: The Search for New Resources

Historically, resource wars are quite common. Asymmetry in the holdings of natural resources has been shown to lower the peace-building effects of bilateral trade.[1] Inability to reach an agreement to fairly divide natural resources that are disputed has been posited as contributing to conflict.[2] The relationship between resources and war holds for civil wars and interstate wars. This chapter focuses on interstate wars. Much of the literature focuses on oil, but other resources also have the potential to cause conflict.[3]

Context: Resources and Their Links to War

There are numerous pathways from scarce resources—notably oil—to international conflict. A variety of other resources are related to conflict, often civil war.[4] Resources that can be exploited and moved

---

[1] Morelli and Sonno, 2017.

[2] Matthew O. Jackson and Massimo Morelli, "The Reasons for Wars: An Updated Survey," in Christopher J. Coyne and Rachel L. Mathers, eds., *The Handbook on the Political Economy of War*, Cheltenham, UK, and Northampton, Mass.: Edward Elgar, 2011, Chapter 3.

[3] Michelle R. Garfinkel and Stergios Skperdas, "Economics of Conflict: An Overview," in Todd Sandler and Keith Hartley, eds., *Handbook of Defense Economics*, Vol. 2, Amsterdam: Elsevier B.V., 2007, Chapter 22.

[4] For a review of the relationship between resources and civil war, see Christopher Blattman and Edward Miguel, "Civil War," *Journal of Economic Literature*, Vol. 48, No. 1, March 2010.

easily by individuals or small groups—resources that can be termed *lootable*, such as diamonds and coltan—can both fuel and finance civil wars.[5] Oil is also associated with civil war, but it is less easily looted or transported in large quantities without attracting attention and countermeasures.

Oilfields can be a target of war, or oil revenues can fund war. An example of the first is the Iraqi invasion of Kuwait in 1990, when Iraq fought for control of oil reserves. An example of the second is the funding of Hezbollah by Iran, made possible by Iranian oil revenues. Of 21 interstate wars that occurred from 1973 to 2007, nine had some causal link to oil.[6]

It is possible to quantify the effects of oil on war. One analysis of 153 countries from 1947 to 2001 found that oil states were about 30 percent more likely to be involved in militarized disputes when oil prices were at $60 per barrel than when they were at $20 per barrel.[7] That result did not hold for other states. The oil price and war relationship was especially true for countries led by revolutionary leaders, those whose ascent was accompanied by some type of violence and who then implemented major policy changes, such as a change in the constitution. Revolutionary leadership makes a difference across a broad range of prices. Oil states were no more likely to go to war than other states at prices below $30 per barrel, but this was not true of revolutionary oil states. Having a revolutionary leader had no effect on going to war only

---

[5] World Bank, *World Development Report 2011: Conflict, Security, and Development*, Washington, D.C., 2011. Coltan is a combination of two minerals often found together in nature: niobium, once known as columbium, and tantalum. They have properties of hardness, conductivity, and resistance to corrosion; niobium is used for high-strength steel alloys and tantalum is used for electronic capacitors (Klaus J. Schulz, Nadine M. Piatak, and John F. Papp, "Niobium and Tantalum," in Klaus J. Schulz, John H. DeYoung, Jr., Robert R. Seal II, and Dwight C. Bradley, eds., *Critical Mineral Resources of the United States—Economic and Environmental Geology and Prospects for Future Supply*, Washington, D.C.: U.S. Geological Survey, U.S. Department of the Interior, Professional Paper 1802—M, 2017, Chapter M).

[6] Jeff D. Colgan, "Fueling the Fire: Pathways from Oil to War," *International Security*, Vol. 38, No. 2, Fall 2013.

[7] Cullen S. Hendrix, *Oil Prices and Interstate Conflict Behavior*, Washington, D.C.: Peterson Institute for International Economics, Working Paper 14-3, July 2014.

once prices topped $70 per barrel (although oil price itself did make a difference).

Evidence suggests that the geography of oil, not just the presence of oil, makes a difference in the incidence of war. Among a set of 606 contiguous countries the average incidence of conflict between 1946 and 2008 was 5.7 percent. When no oil was present in either country, the incidence dropped to 3.1 percent. The presence of oil almost always raised the probability of war relative to the no-oil condition. However, the *location* of the oil resources proved important. Incidence of war was especially high when one country had oil close to the border, suggesting a quick grab was tempting for an aggressor country.[8] Only when one country had oil at the maximum distance from the border was the probability of war lower than the no-oil case (Figure 5.1).

Figure 5.1
Oil and the Probability of Conflict

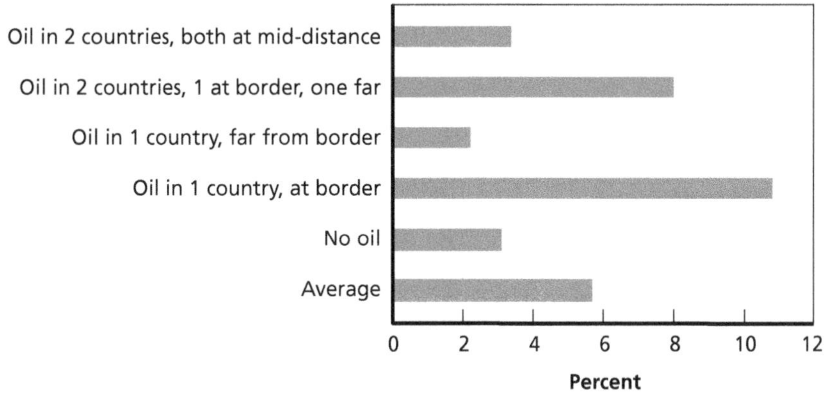

SOURCE: Caselli, Morelli, and Rohner, 2013.

[8] Francesco Caselli, Massimo Morelli, and Dominic Rohner, *The Geography of Interstate Resource Wars*, Washington, D.C.: National Bureau of Economic Research, NBER Working Paper No. 18978, April 2013. Contiguity is defined as sharing a land or river border, or separation by up to 400 miles of water.

Historical Trend: Scarce Resources and International Tensions

Natural resources, particularly oil, have played an important role in U.S. security planning since World War II and have even drawn the United States into war. Notably, these instances did not involve the United States fighting to control resources. Generally, they involved the United States taking action to ensure the flow of oil to allies or to ensure that world markets were not seriously disrupted.

The United States took an early step in January 1953 linking security to resources in response to an antitrust investigation into international oil companies and events in Iran in which democratically elected Prime Minister Mohammed Mosaddegh nationalized that country's oil before being overthrown in a coup. A report to the National Security Council by the Departments of State, Defense, Interior, and Justice noted that the only sources of imported oil for Europe and the United States—"the free world"—were the Middle East and Venezuela.[9] The report also noted that access to oil would be absolutely vital in wartime and that, as a result, "nothing can be allowed to interfere substantially with the availability of oil from those sources to the free world."[10] Produced at the end of the Truman administration, the contents of the document were adopted by the Eisenhower administration, which took office in 1953.[11]

The United States took a more overt step toward promising military action to protect resource flows with the so-called Carter Doctrine, enunciated in President Jimmy Carter's State of the Union speech on

---

[9] U.S. Department of State, U.S. Department of Defense, U.S. Department of Interior, and U.S. Department of Justice, *Report to the National Security Council by the Departments of State, Defense, the Interior, and Justice*, Washington, D.C., NSC 138/1, January 6, 1953 (via Office of the Historian, U.S. Department of State).

[10] U.S. Department of State, U.S. Department of Defense, U.S. Department of Interior, and U.S. Department of Justice, 1953.

[11] Leonardo Maugeri, *The Age of Oil: The Mythology, History, and Future of the World's Most Controversial Resource*, Westport, Conn., and London: Praeger, 2006.

January 23, 1980.[12] A global oil shock followed the Iranian revolution of 1979, and the Soviet Union invaded Afghanistan in December that same year. President Carter in his address noted that this put the Soviet Union in the region that contained two-thirds of the world's potential oil exports and that it put Soviet troops within 300 miles of the Strait of Hormuz, through which most of the world oil exports flowed. The chief U.S. concern was that the Soviet Union would take advantage of any unrest in the region to cause further destabilization, and such destabilization could serve as the rationale for Soviet military action.[13]

Because of this threat and the importance of oil, President Carter announced that

> [a]n attempt by any outside force to gain control of the Persian Gulf region will be regarded as an assault on the vital interests of the United States of America, and such an assault will be repelled by any means necessary, including military force.[14]

Protection of oil resources finally did lead to war, although it was not the Iranians or the Soviet Union that sparked conflict—and, as before, it was not to gain resources for the United States. On August 2, 1990, troops from Iraq, then ruled by Saddam Hussein, invaded Kuwait and conquered it in two days. The first National Security Council meeting in response to the invasion identified the vulnerability of the Kingdom of Saudi Arabia as the top security question: Iraq now had access to 20 percent of global oil reserves and the conquest of Saudi Arabia would double that number. The Saudis, too, had no doubt they were under threat from Iraq.[15] On August 8, President George H. W. Bush announced the movement of U.S. troops to the region and subsequently

---

[12] White House, *State of the Union Address Delivered Before a Joint Session of the Congress*, January 23, 1980.

[13] Melvyn P. Leffler, "From the Truman Doctrine to the Carter Doctrine: Lessons and Dilemmas of the Cold War," *Diplomatic History*, Vol. 7, No. 4, October 1983.

[14] White House, 1980.

[15] Lawrence Freedman and Efraim Karsh, *The Gulf Conflict 1990–1991: Diplomacy and War in the New World Order*, Princeton, N.J.: Princeton University Press, 1993.

assembled a broad military coalition.[16] Military combat operations began on January 17, 1991, and ended with Iraq leaving Kuwait on February 26 and a suspension of coalition operations on February 28.

Serving as architect and guarantor of the international system provided incentive for the United States to create these policies and, ultimately, go to war. Although current U.S. rivals and adversaries have engaged in war, control of resources has not played a significant role in sparking those wars. However, oil revenues have helped fuel wars involving Iran, including the Iran-Iraq war starting in 1980 and the financing of Hezbollah in the Israel-Lebanon war of the 1980s and afterward.[17]

Resources other than oil have also caused tensions, although such tensions have fallen short of causing interstate wars to the extent that oil has. For example, disputes over water in the Aral Sea basin, formed by the Amu Darya and Syr Darya rivers in Central Asia, led to tensions among downstream Uzbekistan and Turkmenistan and upstream Tajikistan and Kyrgyzstan.[18]

Likewise, control over *rare earth elements*, a group of 17 elements that includes scandium, yttrium, and the lanthanides, has caused tensions.[19] China is by far the dominant producer of these elements, which are used in a variety of products and processes, such as magnets, batteries, and polishing. Following a dispute about the Japanese detention of the captain of a Chinese fishing trawler, China withheld exports of rare earth elements in apparent violation of WTO agreements.[20] Notably, China denied it was withholding exports; doing so might have

---

[16] Joseph P. Engelhardt, *Desert Shield and Desert Storm: A Chronology and Troop List for the 1990–1991 Persian Gulf Crisis*, Carlisle, Pa.: Strategic Studies Institute, U.S. Army War College, SSI Special Report AD-A234 743, March 25, 1991.

[17] Colgan, 2013.

[18] Shavkat Kasymov, "Disputes over Water Resources: A History of Conflict and Cooperation in Drainage Basins," *Peace and Conflict Studies*, Vol. 18, No. 2, Article 5, November 1, 2011.

[19] U.S. Geological Survey, "Rare Earths: Statistics and Information," webpage, March 30, 2018.

[20] Keith Bradsher, "Amid Tension, China Blocks Vital Exports to Japan," *New York Times*, September 22, 2010.

given grounds for a WTO dispute.[21] Even before that, China had been tightening its quotas on the export of rare earth elements, leading the United States to eventually file a case in the WTO in cooperation with the EU and Japan. In 2014, the WTO dispute settlement panel found in favor of the U.S. position. China and the United States then notified the WTO in 2015 that they had agreed on procedures for implementing the ruling.[22] While resource disputes can cause international tensions, there has been little evidence so far of them being important causes of war other than oil. However, it is not out of the question that the United States could be drawn into a future war over resources. This is especially true if other great powers use aggression against allies to control resources or otherwise constrain resource flows in an effort to damage world markets.

Future Projection: Access to Resources Poses Vulnerability

Any number of resources are candidates for sparking interstate tensions. One frequently mentioned resource is shared river basins. However, there is little evidence that water has sparked actual war in the post–World War II era.[23] Looking to the future, water remains a concern, especially in Asia, where the ten major river systems originate from the Tibetan plateau.[24] Diversion of this water could have negative effects on downstream neighbors.[25] Water scarcity, fears of denial of access to resources, political instability, and links between water inse-

---

[21] Michael Allan McCrae, "China Denies Withholding Rare Earth Metals from Japan," Mining.com, September 23, 2010.

[22] U.S. Trade Representative, "United States Wins Victory in Rare Earths Dispute with China: WTO Report Finds China's Export Restraints Breach WTO Rules," press release, March 26, 2014; WTO, "DS431: China—Measures Related to the Exportation of Rare Earths, Tungsten and Molybdenum," webpage, May 20, 2015b.

[23] Marit Brochmann and Nils Petter Gleditsch, "Shared Rivers and Conflict—A Reconsideration," *Political Geography*, Vol. 31, No. 8, November 2012.

[24] Jin H. Pak, "China, India, and War over Water," *Parameters*, Vol. 46, No. 2, Summer 2016.

[25] Brahma Chellany, "China Is Stealthily Waging a Water War," *Toronto Globe and Mail*, January 12, 2018.

curity and national sovereignty all could lead to conflict, particularly between China and India.[26]

Whether there are resources that the United States would be compelled to go to war over is an open question. On first glance, oil is a receding candidate. Because of changes in oil and gas extraction technology, the United States has become the second-largest producer of oil in the world.[27] However, the United States is likely to remain an oil importer. Furthermore, U.S. security guarantees and oil-related military actions were not about the security of U.S. supplies; rather, they were generally about disruptions to global markets. Therefore, as long as oil remains important to the world economy, future oil-related wars are possible.

Beyond oil, several other resources might be important. Incidents with rare earth elements point to potential vulnerabilities, as described. Among other resources, cobalt serves as an essential material for rechargeable lithium-ion batteries, used in laptops, smartphones, and electric vehicles, and demand is likely to rise as more electric vehicles take to the road, unless there is a change in battery technology.[28] More than half of the world's cobalt supply comes from Congo, and although new discoveries are taking place elsewhere, it is likely that Congo will remain the key supplier.[29] Furthermore, China has locked in considerable supplies through contracts and has 90 percent of global refining capacity, potentially giving it market power.[30]

---

[26] Pak, 2016.

[27] Robert S. Kaplan, "A Perspective on Oil," Federal Reserve Bank of Dallas, June 19, 2018.

[28] Scott Patterson and Russell Gold, "There's a Global Race to Control Batteries—and China Is Winning," *Wall Street Journal*, February 11, 2018.

[29] Jason Deign, "Reliance on Congo Cobalt Grows Despite European Discoveries," GTM: Greentech Media, June 5, 2018.

[30] On supply being locked in, see Henry Sanderson, "China Tightens Grip on Global Cobalt Supplies," *Financial Times*, March 14, 2018a. On China's refining capacity, see International Energy Agency, *Global EV Outlook 2018: Towards Cross-Modal Electrification*, Paris, 2018.

In response to increasing demand, Congo has revised its mining law to gain a greater share of revenues.[31] But this is a far cry from withholding resources or otherwise blocking access, and international mining companies have the lead role in mining. Even with the market concentration, price volatility in cobalt suggests it is still subject to market forces.[32] Furthermore, there are major efforts to create batteries that do not depend on cobalt.[33] The combination of functioning markets, efforts to increase supply, and efforts to create alternative technologies suggests that a war over cobalt involving the United States is highly unlikely.

In December 2017, President Trump issued an executive order stating that dependence on foreign sources of minerals indicates a strategic vulnerability for the U.S. economy and armed forces, and noted that the United States actually had significant deposits that were not being exploited.[34] He called on the Secretary of the Interior to publish a list of critical minerals and said it would be the policy of the United States to reduce the vulnerability to supply disruptions, largely by increasing domestic supply.

In February 2018, the Department of Interior issued a draft list that included 35 minerals (or groups of minerals, such as rare earth elements) and identified each one's top global producer (the country with the highest level of output) and top U.S. supplier (the country that sold the most to the United States). China was the top producer for 19 of these minerals and the top supplier for 12.[35] The United States was the top producer for two: beryllium, used in satellite communications and other aerospace applications, and helium, used for magnetic resonance

[31] "Revision of Democratic Republic of Congo's Mining Code Driven by Cobalt Price Rise," Dentons, July 2, 2018.

[32] Pratima Desai, "Battery Chemical Surplus Sparks Plunge in Cobalt Price," Reuters, July 31, 2018.

[33] Henry Sanderson, "Electric Cars: The Race to Replace Cobalt," *Financial Times*, August 20, 2018b.

[34] White House, 2017c.

[35] U.S. Department of the Interior, Office of the Secretary, "Draft List of Critical Minerals," *Federal Register*, Vol. 83, No. 33, February 16, 2018.

imaging. After receiving 435 public comments, the Department finalized the list in May with the same 35 minerals.[36]

The desire of the United States to increase domestic production of resources has emerged in other ways. In July 2018, the U.S. Department of Commerce announced an investigation into whether uranium ore and product imports threatened national security.[37] If it turns out that they do, the United States could levy tariffs, and the resulting price increases would encourage domestic producers to increase their output.

Historically, threat of a cutoff to raw materials has contributed to conflict.[38] But just because something is useful to an economy does not mean it will be a flashpoint in war. Earlier work identified 14 raw and semifinished materials that were important to the U.S. economy, with China the controlling producer of 11 of them. This research recommended several steps to mitigate or prepare for supply disruptions, such as increasing resiliency through diversification of production and processing and development of new methods of extraction, processing, and manufacturing. The research also recommended a more robust early warning system.[39]

When materials become scarce and prices rise, economies adjust, which is the largest mitigating factor against resource wars. Either processes change or high prices bring out new supplies. Even now, with concerns about rare earth elements, the United States could increase its own domestic supplies, and Japan in early 2018 reported the discovery of large seabed deposits in its territorial waters about 1,150 miles southeast of Tokyo and far from China.[40]

---

[36] U.S. Department of the Interior, "Final List of Critical Minerals 2018," *Federal Register*, Vol. 83, No. 97, May 18, 2018.

[37] U.S. Department of Commerce, Office of Public Affairs, "U.S. Department of Commerce Initiates Section 232 Investigation into Uranium Imports," Washington, D.C., press release, July 18, 2018.

[38] Robbins, 1968.

[39] Richard Silberglitt, James T. Bartis, Brian G. Chow, David L. An, and Kyle Brady, *Critical Materials: Present Danger to U.S. Manufacturing*, Santa Monica, Calif.: RAND Corporation, RR-133-NIC, 2013.

[40] Yutaro Takaya, Kazutaka Yasukawa, Takehiro Kawasaki, Koichiro Fujinaga, Junichiro Ohta, Yoichi Usui, Kentaro Nakamura, Jun-Ichi Kimura, Qing Chang, Morihisa Hamada,

Implications for the U.S. Air Force and the Future of Warfare

Despite concern about scarcity of resources, there are three broad reasons to think that resource wars—in the sense of wars to control resources or keep others from controlling them—will be rare. First, wars over resources other than oil have not been especially common. And U.S. involvement in wars related to oil has been more about ensuring the flow of supplies to world markets than U.S. ownership of oil or the flow of supplies to the United States. Second, unlike in the immediate post–World War II era, nearly all resources are traded internationally in functioning markets, and obtaining resources has generally been cheaper and more reliable through markets than through conquest.[41] Even creating special relationships to gain access has not necessarily resulted in supply security, as China has experienced with Venezuela.[42] Third, if resources become expensive or difficult to access, technological change or other forms of substitution can often mitigate the scarcity.

There are several risks of future resource wars to consider, but all are low. The first is if a dominant producer tries to withhold supplies for an extended period. For most resource producers, this will be difficult because they need the resource revenues to fund their governments. The second is if a coalition attempts to withhold resources from a third country. The third is if a great power determines that conquering the source nation of a resource is cheaper or more efficient than just buying the resource on the market.

To respond to any of these risks, it would be of value to monitor supply sources and market structure for important resources. Particu-

---

Gjergj Dodbiba, Tatsuo Nozaki, Koichi Iijima, Tomohiro Morisawa, Takuma Kuwahara, Yasuyuki Ishida, Takao Ichimura, Masaki Kitazume, Toyohisa Fujita, and Yasuhiro Kato, "The Tremendous Potential of Deep-Sea Mud as a Source of Rare-Earth Elements," *Nature*, April 10, 2018; Mayumi Negishi, "Japan Hopes Rare-Earth Find Will Give It an Edge Against China," *Wall Street Journal*, April 11, 2018.

[41] David G. Victor, "What Resource Wars?" *The National Interest*, November 12, 2007.

[42] Corina Pons, "Exclusive: Venezuela Faces Heavy Bill as Grace Period Lapses on China Loans—Source," Reuters, April 27, 2018.

lar interest should be given to whether there are dominant suppliers, whether there are alternate sources of supply, and whether there is ability to substitute. A warning sign would be an attempt to withhold supplies over a sustained period of time or to establish exclusive rights to supplies in such a way that the global market would be impaired.

Beyond monitoring, DoD and USAF proactively hedge against cutoffs and shortages though the current National Defense Stockpile, run by the Defense Logistics Agency (DLA).[43] With its roots in an early stockpile created just before World War II, the Stockpile held $1.15 billion worth of 37 types of materials as of September 30, 2016.[44] Each year, the DLA creates an annual materials plan for acquisitions and disposals. For fiscal year 2019 (October 2018 through September 2019), the acquisition plan targeted 19 types of materials and the disposal plan targeted 15 types of materials for potential disposal.[45] Ongoing USAF engagement with the DLA can ensure that Air Force needs are fully met, and USAF engagement with the U.S. Congress can ensure that the Stockpile is appropriately funded to meet DoD and USAF needs and contingencies.

---

[43] U.S. Department of Defense, *Strategic and Critical Materials Operations Report to Congress: Operations Under the Strategic and Critical Materials Stock Piling Act During Fiscal Year 2016*, Washington, D.C.: Defense Logistics Agency Strategic Materials, Office of the Under Secretary of Defense for Acquisition, Technology, and Logistics, January 2017. This is not the only stockpile in the United States. Following an Arab oil cutoff and subsequent price shock in 1973, the United States created the strategic petroleum reserve of up to 713.5 million barrels to be used in times of an energy emergency. U.S. Department of Energy, Office of Fossil Energy, "Strategic Petroleum Reserve," webpage, undated.

[44] More recently, DLA reported that the Stockpile stores 42 commodities at six locations and is valued at more than $1.1 billion. Defense Logistics Agency Strategic Materials, "Our Offices," webpage, undated.

[45] Defense Logistics Agency Strategic Materials, "Annual Materials Plan for FY 2019," [Potential Disposals], DLA-SM-18-3151, October 3, 2018a; Defense Logistics Agency Strategic Materials, "Annual Materials Plan for FY 2019," [Acquisitions], DLA-SM-18-3152, October 3, 2018b.

CHAPTER SIX

Trend 5: The Shrinking Defense Industrial Base

The DIB underlies the ability to develop, produce, and sustain the quantity and quality of warfighting materiel necessary. Since the end of the Cold War, waves of mergers and acquisitions (M&A) have fundamentally altered global DIBs, particularly in the United States and Europe. These consolidations have shrunk the production line capacity and resiliency of producers of complex weapon systems.[1] Our research was conducted for USAF, so this chapter considers the effects of these trends on the health of the fighter aircraft industry in particular, but we note that similar trends are observable in other critical areas of the DIB, such as shipbuilding and munitions.

These trends could harm the ability of the United States to maintain readiness and surge production in response to a major interstate conflict, especially in the unlikely event that one evolved into an extended conventional conflict. They also could limit diversity of materiel when different characteristics might be desirable in different warfighting scenarios. Furthermore, the future DIB workforce could experience challenges—particularly a skills gap, as we will discuss—a situation largely outside of DoD's direct control.

---

[1] We note that trends in consolidation and declines in the number of firms might not be perfectly correlated with declines in production line capacity. However, a recent DoD report explicitly noted production line shutdowns and smaller capabilities in at least one sector. Office of the Secretary of Defense, *Fiscal Year 2017 Annual Industrial Capabilities Report to Congress*, Washington, D.C., March 2018, p. 81.

Context: U.S. Defense Industrial Base Is Healthy, Not Infallible

The health of the U.S. DIB is a thoroughly studied national security subject. In 2015, for instance, RAND Project AIR FORCE conducted an analysis of hundreds of DIB studies published over the past 60 years, focusing on those specific to the aircraft industrial base.[2] It found four persistent concerns in the literature regarding the health of the DIB, all of which have been compounded at least in part by post–Cold War trends in the consolidation of the DIB. These recurring themes focused on the ability of the DIB to do the following:

- surge production capacity in times of crisis—particularly in the event of large-scale interstate conflict, as occurred during World War II—in an era of fewer defense contractors and reduced national manufacturing capacity
- sustain existing weapon systems both in peacetime periods of declining defense budgets and in wartime periods of high maintenance and replacement, the fluctuations between which often drive sub-tier suppliers and producers from the market
- innovate research and design of new systems and technologies, especially given significant market challenges, such as reduced competition because of market consolidation through corporate M&A, declines in supply of advanced manufacturing jobs, and labor market shortfalls in critical engineering and manufacturing skills (particularly among younger workers)
- provide the U.S. government with good value for taxpayer dollars, especially given the reduction in competition between prime contractors.

This comprehensive literature review also found consistency in the assessment—asserted in times of both increasing and decreasing defense spending—that the current state of the U.S. DIB generally and the aircraft industry more narrowly could be characterized as "healthy"

---

2 John Ausink, Michael Thirtle, Rena Rudavsky, and Tony Starkey, unpublished RAND research, 2015.

and meeting the defense needs of the nation, but that future problems could be anticipated.[3] These views are echoed in the U.S. Office of the Secretary of Defense's *Fiscal Year 2017 Annual Industrial Capabilities Report to Congress*, which concludes, "The defense sector continues to financially outperform the broader U.S. equity market. . . . However factors such as obsolescence, foreign dependency, fluctuating demand, industry consolidations, and loss of design teams and manufacturing skills for critical defense products continue to threaten the health of the industrial base, limit innovation, and reduce U.S. competitiveness in the global markets."[4]

Historical Trend: Consolidation and a Defense Industrial Base at Risk

The end of the Cold War brought a profound change to the landscape of DIBs across the world. As global defense spending plummeted, M&A waves, layoffs, and firms exiting the market consolidated the industry at the levels of prime contractors and of first- and second-tier subcontractors. Indeed, of the top 100 global defense companies that existed in 1991, only 19 firms survived to 2014.[5]

This contraction was particularly rapid in the United States following the end of the Cold War. Between 1990 and 1998, the number of contractors making up the top two-thirds of the U.S. defense industry declined by 60 percent.[6] The largest of these consolidations occurred between 1994 and 1997 with the mergers of Northrop and Grumman (1994), Lockheed and Martin Marietta (1995), Boeing and

---

3 John Ausink, Michael Thirtle, Rena Rudavsky, and Tony Starkey, unpublished RAND research, 2015.

4 Office of the Secretary of Defense, 2018, p. 2.

5 Marjorie Censer, "Defense Companies Brace for a Different Kind of Consolidation This Time Around," *Washington Post*, January 12, 2014.

6 Mark Lorell, Julia Lowell, Richard M. Moore, Victoria Greenfield, and Katia Vlachos-Dengler, *Going Global? U.S. Government Policy and the Defense Aerospace Industry*, Santa Monica, Calif.: RAND Corporation, MR-1537-AF, 2002, p. 4.

McDonnell Douglas (1997), and Raytheon and Hughes (1997).[7] These mergers were at least in part encouraged by DoD in 1993 as a defensive measure in response to upcoming department budget cuts.[8] By the early 2000s, General Dynamics emerged as the fifth giant prime after its acquisitions of numerous first- and second-tier subcontractors.[9] Between the early 1980s and early 2000s, the Pentagon's 50 largest suppliers were consolidated into these five contractors.[10]

The march toward consolidation was especially stark in the aircraft industrial base, as DoD's annual procurement of new aircraft declined from a high of about 450 in 1986 to less than 100 throughout the 1990s.[11] In the decades following World War II, more than a dozen firms built military aircraft; by the end of the Cold War, only seven companies were qualified to do so.[12] Following the consolidation in the early 1990s, however, only three prime contractors (Boeing, Lockheed Martin, and Northrop Grumman) remained capable of manufacturing

---

[7] Each of these megamergers was preceded or followed by multiple other major acquisitions during 1990s, including DIB divisions of General Dynamics, General Electric, and Loral (including Unisys and IBM Federal Systems) by Lockheed and Martin; of Rockwell International and Litton by Boeing and McDonnell Douglas; of E-Systems, Chrysler, Texas Instruments, Magnavox, CAE Link, and General Dynamics by Raytheon and Hughes; and of Vought, Westinghouse, LTV Aircraft, and Loral by Northrop and Grumman. John Mintz, "How a Dinner Led to a Feeding Frenzy," *Washington Post*, July 4, 1997; Charles Bagli, "Two Giants Join a Merger Parade in Arms Industry," *New York Times*, July 4, 1997.

[8] Mintz, 1997.

[9] General Dynamics' key acquisitions throughout the 1990s and 2000s included Bath Iron Works, National Steel & Shipbuilding Company, Lockheed's armaments units, Gulfstream Aerospace, Galaxy Aerospace, Advanced Technology Products, General Motors Defense, and Spectrum Astro. Mark Thompson, "The Defense Dinosaurs," *Time*, September 29, 2011.

[10] Greg Schneider and Renae Merle, "Reagan's Defense Buildup Bridged Military Eras," *Washington Post*, June 9, 2004.

[11] Lorell et al., 2002, p. 3.

[12] Ann Markusen, "The Economics of Defence Industry Mergers and Divestitures," *Economic Affairs*, Vol. 17, No. 4, December 1997, p. 28. John Birkler, Paul Bracken, Gordon T. Lee, Mark A. Lorell, Soumen Saha, and Shane Tierney, *Keeping a Competitive U.S. Military Aircraft Market Aloft: Findings from an Analysis of the Industrial Base*, Santa Monica, Calif.: RAND Corporation, MG-1133-OSD, 2011, p. xvii.

and maintaining complex, fixed-wing manned aircraft (Figure 6.1).[13] In July 1998, these tectonic shifts in U.S. prime contractors effectively came to an end after the federal government blocked Lockheed Martin's attempted takeover of Northrop Grumman.[14] Nonetheless, U.S. defense-related M&A transactions have continued at lower-tier levels, averaging some $45 billion annually since 2000, including spikes of $97 billion and $91 billion in 2016 and 2017, respectively.[15]

The European DIB consolidation followed a slightly different trajectory, unfolding more slowly in the 1990s. The early post–Cold War period was characterized by more-cautious restructuring in Europe's fragmented national defense base: "European consolidation at this

Figure 6.1
Consolidation of U.S. Military Aircraft Prime Contractors, 1960–2010

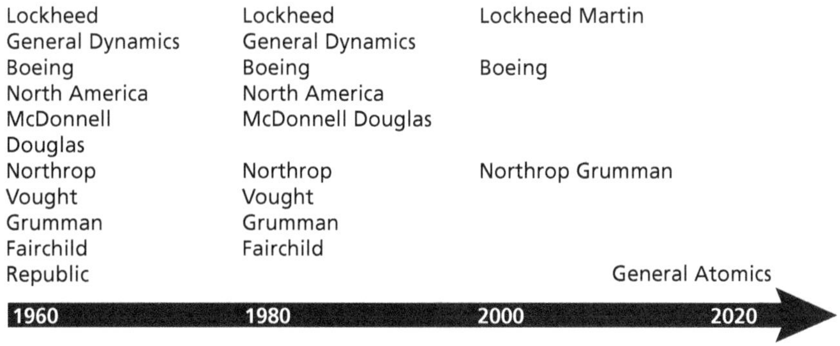

SOURCE: Adapted from Birkler et al., 2011, p. 12.

---

[13] Additionally, General Atomics serves as the only prime contractor for unmanned aerial systems. Similarly, only three major contractors supply large turbofan engines (General Electric, Rolls Royce, and Pratt & Whitney) and avionics (Northrop Grumman, Raytheon, and British Aerospace Systems [BAE]). See Birkler et al., 2011, p. 1.

[14] Leslie Wayne, "Lockheed Cancels Northrop Merger, Citing U.S. Stand," *New York Times*, July 17, 1998.

[15] Three major M&A drove the spikes of 2016 and 2017: Berkshire Hathaway's $32 billion acquisition of Precision Castparts Corp. (2016), United Technologies' pending $30 billion acquisition of Rockwell Collins (2017), and Northrop Grumman's pending $8 billion acquisition of Sparton Corporation (2017). Office of the Secretary of Defense, *Fiscal Year 2016 Annual Industrial Capabilities Report to Congress*, Washington, D.C., March 2017, pp. 103–104; Office of the Secretary of Defense, 2018, p. 27.

time took the form of large national defense champions acquiring small domestic firms . . . or big companies acquiring targets in countries with minor defense industries [but . . .] large-scale cross-border mergers were hindered by the reluctance to see a domestic company acquired by a foreign firm."[16]

By the late 1990s, these trends began to change as the new European Security and Defense Policy gained momentum and as consolidation of the U.S. DIB neared completion. Three European giants were born in 1999 and 2000: BAE Systems, with the merger of British Aerospace and General Electric Company's Marconi Electronic Systems; EADS (now the Airbus Group), with the merger of Aerospatiale Matra, DaimlerChrysler Aerospace (formerly Deutsche Aerospace SA), and Construcciones Aeronauticas SA; and Thales, with Thomson-CSF's acquisition of Racal Electronics.[17] Nonetheless, the process of consolidation in Europe remains incomplete: "[C]ross-border defence consolidation has largely been limited to the air and missile domains";[18] and research, development, testing, and evaluation (RDT&E) and industrial policy continue to be driven largely by fragmented national DIBs despite the post–Cold War creation of such EU frameworks as the European Defence Agency, European Defence Fund, and Permanent Structured Cooperation.[19]

In Russia, post–Cold War DIB restructuring shared some parallels with the West despite occurring against the backdrop of the broader

---

[16] Terrence Guay, *The Transatlantic Defense Industrial Base: Restructuring Scenarios and Their Implications*, Carlisle, Pa.: U.S. Army War College, April 2005, p. 4.

[17] After its incorporation, BAE subsequently acquired four major divisions of Lockheed Martin in 2000: LM Control Systems, LM Aerospace Electronic Systems, LM Space & Electronic Communications, and Sanders Associates & Fairchild Systems. Similarly, EADS subsequently acquired major shares of Dassault Aviation. See Lorell et al., 2002, pp. 4–5; and Guay, 2005, pp. 4–5.

[18] Christina Balis and Henrik Heidenkamp, *Prospects for the European Defence Industrial Base*, RUSI Occasional Paper, September 9, 2014, p. 2.

[19] These observations stem in part from interviews with government officials and researchers in London, Brussels, Berlin, and Warsaw in April 2018. See also *The Future of European Defence: Tackling the Productivity Challenge*, New York: McKinsey and Company, 2013, pp. 10–14 and pp. 24–31.

transition from a command economy to a market-based one. During the Cold War, the Soviet DIB was capable of producing more than 500 fighter aircraft annually; in the 1990s era of declining defense budgets, government demand dropped by more than four-fifths.[20] As in the United States, the fighter aircraft manufacturers consolidated dramatically into two firms, Sukhoi and Mikoyan, which became dependent on foreign exports and contracts in civilian aviation to avoid collapse throughout the 1990s and early 2000s.[21] In February 2006, the aerospace industry was further consolidated when President Vladimir Putin signed a presidential decree creating a new joint-stock company, the United Aircraft Corporation, merging holdings of Mikoyan and Sukhoi with other major fixed-wing and rotary military and civilian aircraft manufacturers, including Ilyshin, Irkut, Tupolev, and Yakovlev; as of 2018, United Aircraft Corporation encompassed some 30 enterprises and remains Russia's largest defense company.[22]

Case Study: Consolidation of Fighter Aircraft Production Lines

Post–Cold War trends in the consolidation of prime contractors have reduced competition and industry capacity, exacerbating enduring vulnerabilities in DIBs' abilities to surge production, sustain existing systems, innovate new platforms, and maximize cost-effectiveness for national governments.[23] The fighter aircraft industry provides an illustrative case study of these dynamics, although the phenomenon is generalizable across DIBs, particularly in other areas of advanced technologies and complex weapon systems. Indeed, as delivery of the F-35A/B/C Joint Fighters has ramped up,[24] U.S. government orders of

---

[20] Christopher Bolkcom and Ellen Schwarzler, *Russian Fighter Aircraft Industrial Base: Parallels with the United States?* Washington, D.C.: Congressional Research Service, RL30730, April 9, 2002, p. 4.

[21] Bolkcom and Schwarzler, 2002, p. 1.

[22] United Aircraft Corporation, "About UAC: History," webpage, undated.

[23] Birkler et al., 2011, p. xvii.

[24] In June 2018, Lockheed Martin marked a milestone by delivering its 300th F-35 to DoD. As of 2019, acquisition plans call for procurement of some 2,456 F-35s. Diane Janeway and Guy Eastman, "US DoD FY19 Budget 'In Depth' Analysis, IHS Jane's, March 15, 2018,

Lockheed Martin and Boeing's four other fourth- and fifth-generation fighter platforms (the F-22 Raptor, F-16 Falcon, F-15 Eagle, and F/A-18E/F Super Hornet) have, to varying degrees, ground to a halt—jeopardizing existing production lines and creating concerns about the industrial base's ability to revitalize them quickly and affordably in the event of a major future conflict.[25] In 2012, the production line of the fifth-generation F-22, which first entered service in 2005, was the first to close permanently after total lifetime deliveries of only 187 aircraft to the Pentagon.[26] Likewise, before 2015, Boeing's F/A-18E/F appeared to be on the path to a pre-2020 retirement until Congress extended its life with new orders in DoD's fiscal year 2016 budget, ensuring its production lines would remain open well into the 2020s.[27] In February 2018, the first new F/A-18E/F to come off Boeing's production line in two years was delivered to the Navy, and DoD's fiscal year 2019 budget request subsequently added an order for 110 new units over fiscal years 2019–2023.[28] In March 2018, Boeing also completed

---

p. 40; Lockheed Martin, "Pentagon and Lockheed Martin Deliver 300th F-35 Aircraft," press release, June 11, 2018.

25 Birkler et al., 2011, pp. 11–24; Mark Arena, John Graser, and Paul DeLuca, *Implications of an Air Force Budget Downturn on the Aircraft Industrial Base: An Exploratory Analysis*, Santa Monica, Calif.: RAND Corporation, RR-248-AF, 2013, p. 14; Valerie Insinna, "Fate of A-10, F-15 to Be Decided This Fall," *Defense News*, September 17, 2017a.

26 "In Focus: End of F-22 Production Closes Chapter in Eventful History," *Flight International*, April 2, 2012. See also Obaid Younossi, Kevin Brancato, John C. Graser, Thomas Light, Rena Rudavsky, and Jerry Sollinger, *Ending F-22A Production: Costs and Industrial Base Implications of Alternative Options*, Santa Monica, Calif.: RAND Corporation, MG-797-AF, 2010.

27 Beatrice Bernardi, John Sneller, Charles Hollosi, Ben Moores, and Mark Bobbi, "Fight-Gen vs. Fourth-Gen: Technology Meets Platform Maturity in a Competing Fighter Market," Jane's Defence Industry & Markets Intelligence Center, October 26, 2017, p. 8. See also Edward G. Keating, Irv Blickstein, Michael Boito, Jess Chandler, and Deborah Peetz, *Evaluating the Desirability of Navy F/A-18E/F Service Life Extension Programs (SLEPs)*, Santa Monica, Calif.: RAND Corporation, TR-844-NAVY, 2010.

28 The fiscal year 2019 budget request also featured a major new Service Life Modification program to modernize more than 350 of the Navy's existing Super Hornet fleet over the next decade. Boeing, "Back to the Future: Boeing Delivers the First Super Hornet to the Navy in Two Years," press release, February 20, 2018a; Boeing, "A Super Hornet Returns to Its Nest: The Boeing Service Life Modification Program Begins," press release, May 7, 2018b.

a long-awaited contract with Kuwait for 28 new F/A-18E/Fs, providing the production line another lifeline.[29]

Similarly, in the absence of any procurement orders from DoD, the struggling production lines of the Pentagon's older fourth-generation workhorses, the F-16 and F-15, have managed to remain open only by attracting new foreign export orders, particularly from governments in the Middle East.[30] In late 2017, Lockheed shuttered its historic Fort Worth, Texas, F-16 production line and moved the F-16's remaining assembly operations to Greenville, South Carolina, as a "temporary measure" to fulfill a new order of 16 aircraft for Bahrain. Pending finalization of another major acquisition deal of 100 to 200 F-16s by the Indian government, Lockheed offered to move the world's only F-16 production line to India.[31] Likewise, although Boeing has not delivered a new F-15 to the Pentagon since the mid-2000s, a recently concluded export order for 36 Eagles to Qatar has helped guarantee that its St. Louis, Missouri, production line will remain open into the 2020s.[32] These future F/A-18E/F, F-15, and F-16 production schedules are modest compared with those of the F-35/A/B/C, but they will temporarily ensure that the mold is not broken on these fourth-generation platforms into the next decade. Nonetheless, the overall effect of DoD's continuing dependence on only two prime contractors and a significant share of single- or sole-source sub-tier suppliers—as well as its planned procurement of only one fighter aircraft model, the F-35, for the foreseeable future—has been to make the aerospace

---

[29] Valeria Insinna, "Boeing and Kuwait Cement Super Hornet Deal," *Defense News*, March 30, 2018.

[30] Marcus Weisgerber, "America's Last Fighter Jet Makers Scramble to Keep Production Alive," *DefenseOne*, May 12, 2016.

[31] As of August 2018, India's order had not been approved. It should be noted that even if this deal is completed, many industry experts do not expect Lockheed to move the F-16's production line to India. Ajai Shukla, "Lockheed Martin Says F-16 Orders Flowing In," Business Standard, December 16, 2017; Chirine Mouchantaf, "Lockheed Keeps F-16 Production Line Going with Bahrain Deal," *Defense News*, January 19, 2018; "F-16 Jet Production in India Will Be Exclusive: Lockheed," *Times of India*, March 19, 2018.

[32] Bernardi et al., 2017, p. 23; Valerie Insinna, "Boeing Scores Big With F-15, KC-46 Contracts with Foreign Militaries," *Defense News*, December 22, 2017c.

industrial base more brittle. As the findings of a recent DoD-led interagency task force summarize: "Production capacity could also become a concern as legacy programs end (F-15, F-16, & F-18) and production lines close. The facilities where these lines are located likely will be refitted for other purposes and space will be occupied with new workload or closed. If this occurs, it will have a limiting effect on industry's ability to surge production in the future."[33] Indeed, in the relatively remote scenario of a great power armed conflict before 2030, an aerospace defense industrial surge would be costly and time-consuming.

In Europe, the production lines of the Eurofighter Typhoon (jointly produced by the United Kingdom, Germany, Italy, and Spain) and, to a lesser extent, the Rafale (produced by France) could suffer similar vulnerabilities in this overlapping period between fourth- and fifth-generation aircraft. The Typhoon was headed for production closure in 2020 until a recent order by Qatar extended its life; no new European demand is expected.[34] The Rafale's future looks somewhat brighter, with deliveries to the French Ministry of Defense on contract and with export orders to India, Qatar, and Egypt over the next decade. Rounding out Europe's fighter industry, the Gripen (produced by Sweden) looks to remain in production for much longer than its European competitors because of its low operating costs and capability equivalence.[35] Likewise, Russia's newest fourth-generation fighters, the MiG-35 and Su-35, are expected to be in production for many years, particularly because of ongoing development problems with United Aircraft Corporation's fifth-generation Su-57 and increased domestic procurement priorities under Russia's latest long-term State Armament Programs (for 2020 and 2027).[36] Among Russia's older fourth-generation aircraft, production

---

[33] DoD, *Assessing and Strengthening the Manufacturing and Defense Industrial Base and Supply Chain Resiliency of the United States*, report to President Donald J. Trump by the Interagency Task Force in Fulfillment of Executive Order 13806, September 2018b, p. 66.

[34] Bernardi et al., 2017, p. 9.

[35] Bernardi et al., 2017, p. 10.

[36] Bernardi et al., 2017, p. 11; Richard Connolly and Mathieu Boulegue, "Russia's New State Armament Programme: Implications for the Russian Armed Forces and Military Capabilities to 2027," London: Chatham House, research paper, May 2018.

of Su-30 variants is expected to be sustained into the 2020s by both domestic and foreign export orders; the long-running lines of the Su-29 and MiG-29 are expected to be retired in the next decade. Table A.1 in the appendix of this report details the world's current major fourth- and fifth-generation fighter aircraft programs by prime contractor and production line status.

Consolidation Elsewhere in the Defense Industrial Base

While the preceding discussion described effects of DIB consolidation on the diversity and resiliency of fighter aircraft production lines, similar trends are observable in other complex manufacturing areas of the DIB, such as munitions production and shipbuilding. As DoD's *Fiscal Year 2017 Annual Industrial Capabilities Report to Congress* acknowledges, for instance, the munitions and missile development and production markets have experienced a significant contraction since the end of the Cold War, and now two prime contractors—Raytheon and Lockheed Martin—account for approximately 97 percent of the Pentagon's procurement in this area.[37] These companies have struggled with capacity constraints as global demand for U.S.-made precision munitions has soared in the prosecution of air campaigns against the Islamic State in Syria and Iraq and against other terrorist and insurgent organizations. USAF Secretary Heather Wilson noted in February 2018 that throughout Operation Inherent Resolve (the operation against the Islamic State), USAF has been using precision munitions "faster than we can make them."[38]

---

[37] While the report concludes that "most or all of the major issues lie within the missile industrial base" as opposed to production capacity for "'dumb' bombs, ammunition, mortars, and tank rounds," it also recognizes that "many of the issues listed for missiles are also applicable to other munitions, especially declining procurement numbers, which have led to production line shutdowns and plants that are being closed into smaller footprints and smaller capabilities." Office of the Secretary of Defense, 2018, pp. 81, 83, 87.

[38] Andrea Shalal, "U.S. Arms Makers Strain to Meet Demand as Mideast Conflicts Rage," Reuters, December 4, 2015; Paul Shinkman, "ISIS War Drains U.S. Bomb Supply," *U.S. News and World Report*, February 17, 2017; John Tirpak, "Munitions Production Surge Planned for At Least Five Years," *Air Force Magazine*, February 22, 2018.

Like the fighter aircraft industry, the missile and munitions industry has also suffered a lack of new system designs over the past two decades, causing the atrophy of vital design skills and a narrowing of indigenous supply chains for critical parts and materials as domestic firms have been forced to exit the market, creating risky dependence on foreign suppliers, such as China.[39] Indeed, in the event of a national emergency, inventories of munitions might be depleted quickly and require long and costly timelines for firms to make necessary production adjustments. In short, trends in the consolidation of the DIB have damaged "the readiness of the Department [of Defense] and negatively [affected] a foundational national defense priority by placing the ballistic missile production capability at risk."[40] These vulnerabilities could have negative consequences not only on the future warfighting ability of the United States, but also on that of key U.S. partners and allies who largely rely on supplies of U.S.-made munitions, including the United Kingdom, France, Italy, South Korea, Saudi Arabia, Pakistan, Lebanon, and the Gulf States.

Likewise, as the total number of active ships in the U.S. Navy's fleet at the end of the Cold War declined from a total of 454 in 1993 to a low of 271 in 2015, the Pentagon concluded that its existing shipbuilding and maintenance capacity significantly exceeded its demand and closed several public shipyards.[41] Today, the U.S. Navy's DIB has been consolidated into just seven shipyards owned by four major contractors and their suppliers: General Dynamics, Huntington Ingalls, Fincantieri, and

---

[39] At the sub-tier level, the *Fiscal Year 2017 Industrial Capabilities Report to Congress* found similar problems in diversity and competition as at the prime level: "A recent study of 35 'key' munitions in production found that the industrial base is dominated by single/sole-source suppliers. For second-tier suppliers, there were 253 critical components (121 suppliers), and 98% of them were single/sole source, and for third-tier suppliers there were 131 critical components (73 suppliers) and 98% were also single/sole source." Office of the Secretary of Defense, 2018, pp. 82–83, 89–90. See also Aaron Mehta, "The US Is Running Out of Bombs—and It May Soon Struggle to Make More," *Defense News*, May 22, 2018.

[40] Office of the Secretary of Defense, 2018, p. 82.

[41] Bradley Martin, Michael E. McMahon, Jessie Riposo, James G. Kallimi, Angelena Bohman, Alyssa Ramos, and Abby Schendt, *A Strategic Assessment of the Future of U.S. Navy Ship Maintenance: Challenges and Opportunities*, Santa Monica, Calif.: RAND Corporation, RR-1951-NAVY, 2017, pp. 1–2.

Austal.[42] At lower tiers of the supply chain, approximately 50 percent of the market for critical materials and parts is dependent on single- or sole-source providers.[43] Significantly, however, the Navy in December 2016 announced a revised 30-year force structure plan to increase its fleet to 355 ships, which might add capability and capacity across the entire shipbuilding value chain and partly reverse post–Cold War trends in declining shipbuilding resiliency. Indeed, because major shipbuilders have maintained hot production lines and are operating at only 70 to 80 percent of capacity, industry leaders are optimistic that they will be able to ramp up over a period of several years to meet this long-term demand increase through the middle of the 21st century.[44] Nonetheless, according to CBO estimates, the shortest amount of time in which the naval DIB could achieve the Navy's desired increase to a fleet of 355 ships is 18 years.[45] As with fighter aircraft and munitions and missile production lines, therefore, in the event of a large-scale conflict, "Navy shipbuilding rates could not be increased steeply across the board overnight—time (and investment) would be needed to hire and train additional workers and increase production facilities at shipyards and supplier firms, particularly for supporting higher rates of submarine production."[46]

---

[42] Office of the Secretary of Defense, 2018, pp. 100–101.

[43] Office of the Secretary of Defense, 2018, p. 100.

[44] Ronald O'Rourke, *Navy Force Structure and Shipbuilding Plans: Background and Issues for Congress*, Washington, D.C.: Congressional Research Service, RL32665, July 31, 2018, pp. 9, 90–99. See also John P. Casey, "Testimony of John P. Casey before the Senate Armed Services Committee, Subcommittee on Seapower, 115th Congress, Supporting the 355-Ship Navy with Focus on Submarine Industrial Base," Washington, D.C., May 24, 2017; Brian Cuccias, "Statement of Brian Cuccias, President, Ingalls Shipbuilding, Huntington Ingalls Industries, Subcommittee on Seapower, Senate Armed Services Committee, 115th Congress," Washington, D.C., May 24, 2017; Matthew O. Paxton, "Testimony of Matthew O. Paxton, President, Shipbuilders Council of America, before the United States Senate Committee on Armed Services, Subcommittee on Seapower, [on] Industry Perspectives on Options and Considerations for Achieving a 355-Ship Navy," Washington, D.C., May 24, 2017.

[45] CBO, *Costs of Building a 355-Ship Navy*, Washington, D.C., April 2017, p. 1.

[46] O'Rourke, 2018, p. 9.

Future Projection: U.S. Dominance Vulnerable to Foreign and Domestic Challenges

The health of the overall U.S. DIB is likely to be marked by several future trends. First, U.S. production capacity likely will continue to exceed that of its near-competitors through the middle of the 2020s. Among the top 100 defense firms worldwide, excluding China, U.S. firms accounted for the majority of sales from 2002 to 2016 (62 percent on average), and there is no reason to anticipate a change in this trend.[47] This dominance is particularly true in the fighter aircraft industry, where the F-35 is expected to account for some 30 percent to 40 percent of all new global aircraft through 2026 (Figure 6.2). Indeed, according to one industry analysis, "That dominance will continue far

Figure 6.2
Projected Future Deliveries of Major Fourth- and Fifth-Generation Fighter Aircraft, 2017–2026

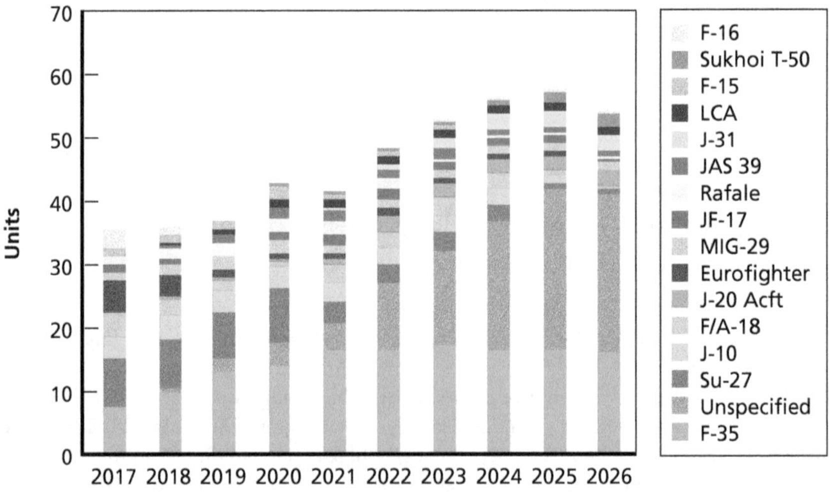

SOURCE: Bernardi et al., 2017, p. 14.

---

[47] Sales from 2002 to 2016 are based on data from Stockholm International Peace Research Institute, *SIPRI Arms Industry Database*, Solna, Sweden, 2017. The top 100 firms are from the United States, the EU, non-U.S. NATO, Russia, Australia, Brazil, India, Israel, Japan, Kuwait, Singapore, South Africa, South Korea, and Ukraine.

beyond the forecast period."[48] This projection might prove particularly true as unit costs of the F-35 continue to decline and Lockheed potentially wins more export contracts.

Second, within the aerospace DIB specifically, the fourth-generation U.S. fighter aircraft production lines might atrophy over the next decade despite the positive outlook for the F-35's production lines. Those in Europe, Russia, and China could experience similar pressures but are likely to stay online well beyond U.S. fourth-generation fighters because of the slower development of fifth-generation platforms and greater export demand relative to domestic demand in those countries. With no new manned fighter programs in planning or development as of mid-2018, the United States could soon be in the position of having the F-35 as its only active domestic fighter aircraft production line and Lockheed Martin as the only prime serving government demand. Because the manufacturing bases of fighters are complex, shutting down fourth-generation production lines without investing to preserve any production capability would make restarting future production expensive and difficult.[49]

Third, sustaining the health of domestic and allied DIBs might become increasingly challenging if U.S. and European defense budgets were to decline and Chinese and Russian defense budgets were to rise concurrently. Spending on procurement and RDT&E has typically come under greater pressure during spending cutbacks than has spending on operations and maintenance and personnel. Moreover, future periods of austerity will differ from previous economic downturns and post–Cold War era defense spending cuts because of the "emergence of a competitor [i.e., China] with significant technical and economic capability."[50] Thus, the United States' relative DIB advantage might narrow throughout the 2020s and 2030s. In Europe, the DIB likely will remain fragmented and dominated by national defense companies, and RDT&E investment and procurement decisions likely will continue to be driven by national decisionmaking rather than inte-

---

48 Bernardi et al., 2017, p. 14.

49 Younossi et al., 2010.

50 Arena, Graser, and DeLuca, 2013, p. xi.

grated efforts, "leading to significant redundancies and inefficiencies in the regional industrial base."[51] At the same time, future spending cuts might create new pressure for subprime consolidation in both the U.S. and European aerospace industries.[52]

Fourth and relatedly, a future security environment in which "inter-state strategic competition, not terrorism, is now the primary concern in U.S. national security" could mean that advanced threats will demand more-capable and more-sophisticated platforms, particularly in fighter aircraft.[53] This forecast implies a greater demand in the aerospace labor market for specialized engineering and technical skills. Worrisomely, the U.S. DIB is confronted by an aging workforce and a shortage of highly skilled, younger, replacement labor.[54] In 2017, 61 percent of workers in aerospace and defense industries were 46 years of age or older.[55] Meanwhile, in 2009, only 1.5 percent of employed Americans in the 25–34 age demographic possessed a science or engineering degree.[56] In the manufacturing industry more broadly, it is estimated that the U.S. economy will demand some 3.5 million manufacturing jobs from 2015 to 2025, but some 2 million of these positions will go unfilled because of the skill gap as baby boomers retire.[57] Moreover, the vast majority of graduate-level students pursuing full-time degrees in critical technology fields at U.S. colleges and universities are foreign nationals unable to obtain U.S. security clearances, including 81 percent in electrical and petroleum engineering, 79 per-

---

51 Balis and Heidenkamp, 2014, p. 4.

52 Paul McLeary, "Defense Industry Running Out of Time; Mergers Loom," *Defense News*, January 9, 2015; Marcus Weisgerber, "Pentagon Worried About Defense Contractor Monopolies," *Fiscal Times*, October 3, 2015.

53 DoD, *Summary of the 2018 National Defense Strategy of the United States of America: Sharpening the American Military's Competitive Edge*, Washington, D.C., 2018a, p. 1.

54 Arena, Graser, and DeLuca, 2013, pp. 14–15.

55 Office of the Secretary of Defense, 2018, p. 8.

56 Organisation for Economic Co-operation and Development, *Education at a Glance 2011*, Paris, 2011, Table A4.6, p. 87.

57 Deloitte and Manufacturing Institute, *The Skills Gap in U.S. Manufacturing: 2015 and Beyond*, New York, 2015, p. 5.

cent in computer science, 75 percent in industrial engineering, 63 percent in mechanical engineering, 59 percent in civil engineering, and 57 percent in chemical engineering.[58] This labor market trend raises serious concerns about U.S. capacity to scale up production of complex weapon platforms, including fighter aircraft, in the event of a major interstate conflict with a near-peer state competitor.

At the same time, however, these U.S. labor market vulnerabilities might be ameliorated partly by parallel trends in the growth of advanced manufacturing processes—such as additive manufacturing (AM), automation, artificial intelligence as applied to manufacturing, and robotics—which are likely be particularly disruptive in the production of high-complexity, high-cost, low-volume goods, including aerospace components.[59] For instance, as the Atlantic Council recently noted, "Low-volume production found in the aerospace industry makes it another market primed for disruption from AM. . . . There exist many instances of AM parts being used in aircraft. One example is an environmental control system duct on the F-18. The complexity offered by AM enabled the redesign of the assembly, and reduced the number of parts involved from sixteen to just one."[60] Proliferation of AM also might mitigate some DIB vulnerabilities arising from market consolidation and persistent M&A by enabling production of discontinued components in the absence of original manufacturers.[61] On

---

[58] National Foundation for American Policy, "The Importance of International Students to American Science and Engineering," Arlington, Va., NFAP Policy Brief, October 2017, p. 1.

[59] Trevor Johnston, Troy D. Smith, and J. Luke Irwin, *Additive Manufacturing in 2040: Powerful Enabler, Disruptive Threat*, Santa Monica, Calif.: RAND Corporation, PE-283-RC, 2018, pp. 8–14. See also Dylan Bell, Jeffrey Fallat, Gregory Sterley, and Ehssan Alsuhibani, *The Future of Additive Manufacturing in the U.S. Military*, Maxwell Air Force Base, Ala.: Air War College, Air University, March 17, 2017; Benjamin D. Forest, *The Future of Additive Manufacturing in Air Force Acquisition*, Maxwell Air Force Base, Ala.: Air War College, Air University, March 22, 2017; and Tuke Klemmt, Rashid Faraby, and Katherine Multop, "Additive Manufacturing: Fundamental Concepts," Washington, D.C., Defense Acquisition University (DAU) briefing, February 7, 2018.

[60] Thomas Campbell, Christopher Williams, Olga Ivanova, and Banning Garrett, *Could 3D Printing Change the World? Technologies, Potential, and Implications of Additive Manufacturing*, Washington, D.C.: Atlantic Council, Strategic Foresight Report, October 2011, p. 4.

[61] Johnston, Smith, and Irwin, 2018, p. 12; Klemmt, Faraby, and Multop, 2018, p. 14.

the other hand, U.S. challengers (such as China) have reportedly also become increasingly interested in integrating AM technologies into their respective DIBs; thus, "at the state level, AM has the potential to level the playing field between competitors and attenuate asymmetric advantages that some nations (e.g., the United States) currently enjoy."[62]

Implications for the U.S. Air Force and the Future of Warfare

These trends in the shrinking DIB hold important implications for USAF, DoD, and U.S. national security objectives more broadly. First, fewer warm production lines for complex, fixed-wing manned aircraft and other critical DIB areas (such as shipbuilding and munitions and missile manufacturing) could harm the ability of the United States to maintain readiness and to surge production in response to an emergency or extended contingencies, especially a major (albeit unlikely) interstate conflict with a near-peer adversary.[63]

This vulnerability is particularly acute today because of both the capital intensity of modern platforms and advanced technologies and the relative declines in U.S. production of raw materials critical to these aerospace and defense systems, such as aluminum, titanium, steel, lead, zinc, and nickel.[64] Whereas U.S. production of fixed and rotary military aircraft surged during World War II from some 2,100 in 1939 to 96,300 in 1944, similar scalability likely would not be possible in the event of full warfare.[65] While other near-peers would experience similar surge challenges, parallel trends in the relative decline of U.S. economic might (specifically in relation to a rising China) likely will exacerbate this vulnerability.

---

[62] Johnston, Smith, and Irwin, 2018, p. 13.

[63] DoD, 2018b, pp. 65–66, 79–80.

[64] Mike Gallagher, "Hedging Our Bets: Reviving Defense Industrial Surge Capacity," *War on the Rocks*, December 1, 2017.

[65] Bill Vogt, "What You Can Do When You Have To," *Target*, Vol. 15, No. 1, First Quarter, 1999, p. 3,

This difficulty of surging production also might have implications for how wars are fought. With lower resilience and a lower ability to replenish weapons, a belligerent challenger fighting the United States might strive for some kind of large-scale attack to knock out U.S. capabilities. Alternatively, a challenger could escalate conflict quickly before the United States and its allies could build new supplies.

Second, the Air Force will encounter difficult trade-offs between efficiency and cost-effectiveness on the one hand and resiliency and redundancy on the other. While DoD's future plans to procure only one or two models of fighter aircraft could provide gains in the former, they might prove shortsighted acquisition strategies in the latter, making the production system brittle and potentially overlooking the desirability of maintaining a diversity of platforms with different cost, production speed, and performance capabilities and advantages.[66] In short, the benefits of closing production lines in terms of financial costs might sometimes be outweighed by strategic costs.[67] Accordingly, as a hedge against the intrinsic unpredictability of the future threat environment, DoD or USAF could mount an explicit long-term effort to preserve a reconstitution capacity for those production lines and segments of the DIB that it considers most likely to be needed in an emergency.[68] DoD

[66] For instance, as the Heritage Foundation notes, the F-22 and F-35 were designed and built to complete many unique and complementary missions. Simply purchasing more of the latter as a substitute for the former is an "insufficient" acquisition equation: "The F-22, a larger and more maneuverable aircraft, was meant to fulfill air dominance missions, thereby clearing the skies for the multi-role strike mission of the F-35. Indeed, this complementary mission set specifically assumed that the F-22 would be available in sufficient quantity to provide air cover for the F-35. Without enough F-22s to eliminate any air-to-air and surface-to-air threats, the F-35 will become increasingly and unnecessarily vulnerable." Mackenzie M. Eaglen and Eric Sayers, *Maintaining the Superiority of America's Defense Industrial Base*, Washington, D.C.: Heritage Foundation, Backgrounder No. 2276, May 22, 2009, p. 6. See also Aerospace Industries Association, *Fostering the Manufacturing & Defense Industrial Base of the Future*, Arlington, Va., April 2018, p. 2.

[67] Mark A. Lorell, Michael Kennedy, Robert S. Leonard, Ken Munson, Shmuel Abramzon, David L. An, and Robert A. Guffey, *Do Joint Fighter Programs Save Money?* Santa Monica, Calif.: RAND Corporation, MG-1225-AF, 2013, pp. 35–37.

[68] John Birkler, Joseph P. Large, Giles K. Smith, and Fred Timson, *Reconstituting a Production Capability: Past Experience, Restart Criteria and Suggested Policies*, Santa Monica, Calif.: RAND Corporation, MR-273-ACQ, 1993.

and Congress could also boost resiliency and redundancy in the U.S. DIB by promoting and incentivizing additional foreign military sales of legacy weapon systems (such as fourth-generation fighter aircraft) rather than newer ones (such as the F-35). Indeed, as the recent experiences of Lockheed and Boeing have demonstrated, even relatively modest foreign sales contracts can be sufficient to preserve production lines and stave off brain drain in industrial areas vital to U.S. national security.

Third, even short of readiness and resiliency concerns in the event of major demand increases, other factors threaten the U.S. DIB's capacity to perform at current output levels. Some of these factors, specifically labor market trends and continued M&A, might increasingly fall outside DoD's direct control. These trends might erode competitive forces, innovation, and high-skill engineering design and technological expertise in the U.S. DIB. On the other hand, proliferation of advanced manufacturing processes and technologies—such as AM, artificial intelligence, automation, and robotics—might in part mitigate some DIB vulnerabilities arising from persistent market consolidation and longer-term labor market trends in industrial manufacturing and in science, technology, engineering, and math education.

CHAPTER SEVEN

Trend 6: Decreasing Power of U.S. Sanctions

Military equipment is a direct tool of warfare and security policy. Sanctions are also a tool, although sometimes less direct, that can be used as a tool in conflict or as a substitute for conflict. In many cases they are preferred to military action because most such measures are not acts of war and pose a low cost to the society instituting them.

A wide variety of economic actions fall under the category of *sanctions*, in which one nation bars certain economic transactions with another. Sanctions should be differentiated from *economic warfare*, or economic actions in war, such as blockading a country or bombing its ports and factories.

Sanctions are not an end in themselves. They can be instituted to achieve four possible outcomes:[1]

1. compliance, to bring about a behavioral or policy change
2. subversion, to destabilize or remove a government or regime
3. deterrence, to stop a country from taking a specific action
4. symbolism, to send a message to an international or even domestic audience.

Generally, they are not meant to be permanent, but to have a specific effect.

The empirical track record suggests that sanctions are more effective if instituted by a dominant economy. Furthermore, they are more

[1] Michael J. Meese, Suzanne C. Nielsen, and Rachel M. Sondheimer, *American National Security*, 7th ed., Baltimore, Md.: Johns Hopkins University Press, 2018.

effective if instituted multilaterally. In peacetime or times of low-level conflict short of war, they can cause significant economic damage and can lead to a changed policy environment, such as by bringing an adversary back to negotiations; however, they rarely lead to major policy changes. In wartime, they rarely lead to victory by themselves, but they can influence the policies of targets, and they can degrade an adversary's capabilities or access to resources.

But they risk being overused, leading to a decline in their power, although such a decline is not yet apparent. And they can breed reaction—countries will attempt to work around the sanctions and to dilute the power of future sanctions. This is especially true of unilateral U.S. sanctions. Multilateral sanctions coordinated with all major economies are likely to remain powerful longer.

Context: Different Types of Sanctions, Different Effects

The most basic economic action a nation can take is to block trade in goods or services. Such trade sanctions can be targeted at a particular sector or a particular country. They can be instituted by a single country or multilaterally. Just as countries can ban trade, they can ban investment, the remittance of investment profits or interest, and the repatriation of capital already invested. For example, in the package of sanctions against Russia following its invasion of Crimea and the subsequent war in Eastern Ukraine, both the United States and the EU banned investment in Crimea. Actions regarding the oil industry effectively blocked new Western investment in deepwater, Arctic, or shale projects in Russia. In August 2017, the United States approved a law expanding the menu of possible investment sanctions.[2]

One contentious aspect of such investment sanctions—and potentially of trade and financial sanctions—is that they can sometimes have extraterritorial effect. For example, if certain provisions in the August 2017 law are instituted, they would affect European com-

[2] Public Law 115-44, Countering America's Adversaries Through Sanctions Act, August 2, 2017.

panies building Nord Stream 2, a gas export pipeline from Russia to Germany.[3]

Related to investment sanctions, financial sanctions block financial relations with the target of the economic action. With the dollar serving as the global reserve currency and the main currency for international trade, the United States is in an unparalleled position to impose financial sanctions. The most invasive step is for the United States to block an institution's access to the U.S. financial system, effectively cutting it off from the international financial system because other banks will be reluctant to do business with it, and largely cutting it off from the use of the dollar to settle international transactions. This effectively blocks it from most trade relations because the U.S. dollar is the most prominent currency for trade settlements, and most dollar transactions have to touch the U.S. financial system at some point.

Decades of empirical analysis provide evidence that sanctions can have serious economic consequences on a target country, especially when smaller countries are the targets. Trade sanctions can decrease trade anywhere from very little to up to about 90 percent.[4] Financial sanctions tend to have more serious effects. One analysis of U.S. sanctions on Iran up to about 2000 found that the annualized total effect of financial and investment sanctions was $637 million dollars for 2000 and 2001, compared with $140 million in losses per year due to trade sanctions.[5] Besides declines in GDP, financial sanctions can cause higher inflation, higher borrowing costs, and capital flight. And almost all analyses show that multilateral sanctions are more effective than unilateral sanctions.[6]

---

3 "Germany Urges EU to Fight Back Against Russia Sanctions Bill," Radio Free Europe/Radio Liberty, August 1, 2017.

4 A good overall review of sanctions can be found in Gary Clyde Hufbauer, Jeffrey J. Schott, Kimberly Ann Elliott, and Barbara Oegg, *Economic Sanctions Reconsidered*, 3rd ed., Washington, D.C.: Peterson Institute for International Economics, 2007.

5 Akbar E. Torbat, "Impacts of the US Trade and Financial Sanctions on Iran," *The World Economy*, Vol. 28, No. 3, 2005.

6 Jiawen Yang, Hossein Askari, John Forrer, and Hildy Teegen, "U.S. Economic Sanctions: An Empirical Study," *International Trade Journal*, Vol. 18, No. 1, Spring 2004.

Historical Trend: Sanctions' Increased Power, Increased Use

Sanctions are certainly as old as warfare in Western civilization: Around 433 B.C., for example, Athens instituted the so-called Megarian decree, which banned people from Megara from using Athenian markets or any ports of the Athenian empire.[7] In the modern era, sanctions originally were instituted with largely military objectives—for example, getting a nation to withdraw its troops after an incursion.[8] After World War II, however, the purpose of sanctions was broadened to include more-general national security and foreign policy goals. In the 1990s, after the Cold War ended, the use of sanctions evolved once again, with the Bill Clinton administration using targeted sanctions against a specific person or company rather than a country.[9]

Just as the purposes of sanctions have broadened, so have U.S. legal authorities. Legal authorities increased in 1976 with the National Emergencies Act and again in 1977 with the International Emergency Economic Powers Act. After declaring a national emergency, the president could cite the 1977 act to employ broad powers in regulating economic activity.[10] But for several years, the United States usually did not impose sanctions on imports because doing so required a finding of a national security threat or other national emergency.[11] It was not until 1985, with the passage of Section 505 of the International Security and Development Cooperation Act, that the United States established legal authority to block imports from countries that support or harbor terrorists or terrorist organizations.

---

[7] Evelyn Abbot, *A History of Greece, Part III: From the Thirty Years' Peace to the Fall of the Thirty at Athens, 445–403 B.C.*, London and Bombay: Longmans, Green and Co., 1900; Ronald P. Legon, "The Megarian Decree and the Balance of Greek Naval Power," *Classical Philology*, Vol. 68, No. 3, July 1973.

[8] Hufbauer et al., 2007.

[9] Juan C. Zarate, *Treasury's War: The Unleashing of a New Era of Financial Warfare*, New York: Public Affairs, 2013.

[10] Catherine Padhi, "Emergencies Without End: A Primer on Federal States of Emergency," *Lawfare*, December 8, 2017.

[11] Hufbauer et al., 2007, p. 45.

The attacks of September 11, 2001, gave rise to significant legal innovation that broadened authorities to make sanctions far more effective than they had been. The focus of these legal innovations was financial sanctions, and they gave the United States much greater ability to cut people, institutions, and nations off from the global financial system. There were three broad lines of effort. The first involved expanding international efforts to halt money-laundering. The second involved expanding financial intelligence and developing new financial tools to track and disrupt illicit financial flows. The third involved effectively enlisting private-sector financial institutions to be more on guard for—and to bear more of the risk if they ignored—illicit financial flows.[12]

Exemplary of this was Section 311 of the USA Patriot Act. Under that section, the Treasury's Financial Crimes Enforcement Network can declare an institution or a country to be of "primary money laundering concern" and then institute one or more of five special measures. Among these is the power to prohibit U.S. financial institutions from maintaining correspondent accounts for the targeted entity, effectively cutting the entity off from using dollars internationally and thereby cutting it off from business around the world.[13] This measure was used against Macao-based Banco Delta Asia in 2005 as a way of cutting off North Korea's access to global finance, and against Iran in 2011.[14]

Future Projection: U.S. Sanctions Powerful, but Not All-Powerful

As long as the United States is central to the global economy, it will be able to use sanctions as a tool to shape other nations' behavior.

---

[12] Zarate, 2013.

[13] Stephen Heifetz and Evan Sherwood, "Those Other Economic Sanctions: Section 311 Special Measures," *The Banking Law Journal*, Vol. 131, No. 9, September 2014.

[14] U.S. Department of the Treasury, "Treasury Designates Banco Delta Asia as Primary Money Laundering Concern Under USA PATRIOT Act," Washington, D.C., Press Release JS-2720, September 15, 2005; U.S. Department of the Treasury, "Fact Sheet: New Sanctions on Iran," Washington, D.C., November 21, 2011.

That centrality comes in two forms. First, the United States is the largest trading nation, by far. In 2017, U.S. trade in total goods and services amounted to $5.2 trillion on a balance-of-payments basis, well ahead of China's $4.6 trillion. This is partly because of high U.S. import demand. Notably, the European Union is well ahead of both, at $15.2 trillion in total goods and services traded. These totals, however, include intra-EU trade.[15]

Although China is a slightly larger exporter, being the largest importer has certain advantages. Denial of opportunities to sell to the importer's market could damage the economy of the country being sanctioned. This also suggests that the United States and Europe combined have more power than either alone.

The second form of centrality is the use of the dollar globally and the importance of the U.S. financial sector to international transactions. For example, U.S. dollars constitute the largest share of global reserves by far, and this has held steady over the long term. In the 33 quarters from the beginning of 2010 through the first quarter of 2018, the U.S. dollar has constituted, on average, 63 percent of global reserves when the currency of those reserves can be identified, ranging from 61 percent to 66 percent.[16]

Among the elements that make the dollar central are history (the United States as the motivator and shaper of the global financial system after World War II), the size of the U.S. economy, and the openness and sophistication of U.S. capital markets. Other economies are unlikely to challenge the United States in the latter two domains in

---

[15] World Bank, 2018.

[16] International Monetary Fund, Currency Composition of Official Foreign Exchange Reserves (COFER), July 2, 2018c. The euro share has been more volatile but has trended downward. It was above 25 percent of reserves in cases for which the currency could be identified through the third quarter of 2011, but stayed within the narrow range of 19 percent to 21 percent from the first quarter of 2015 to the first quarter of 2018. The RMB has been rising, but from a very low base—from zero before the end of 2016 to 1.4 percent in the first quarter of 2018. The IMF's coverage of international reserves has greatly improved. In the first quarter of 2010, the IMF had currency data for only 56 percent of global reserves. By the first quarter of 2018, that had risen to almost 90 percent. Even with that increase, the U.S. dollar share held steady, suggesting that many of the previously unattributed reserves were in dollars.

the next few years, although projecting out to 2030 is more difficult. The European financial sector took longer to return to health than the U.S. financial sector after the global financial crisis; its banks are still more fragmented, and European capital markets are not as deep as those of the United States, providing a U.S. advantage for holders and traders of currencies.[17] By 2030, Europe might have achieved a unified financial market and the euro might be a much more prominent currency in international trade. In contrast, China is unlikely to reform its financial sector and free the RMB to the extent that would be necessary to allow it to become a major international currency—doing so would introduce significant risks to the Chinese economy.[18]

Despite this centrality, the United States is not all-powerful. For example, Western sanctions on Russia have not completely sealed that country off from the transactions that the United States and Europe want to ban. China has not joined in the sanctions, and several Middle Eastern and Asian nations have also engaged in transactions that are off limits to Western companies.[19] China also has been trying to start a new international payments system that would help transactions bypass the U.S. banking system by enabling easier RMB payments, although

---

[17] For information on the European banking and financial sectors, see Nicolas Véron, "EU Financial Services Policy Since 2007: Crisis, Responses and Prospects," *Global Policy*, Vol. 9, Supplement 1, June 2018; and Patty Duijm and Dirk Schoenmaker, "European Bank Mergers: Domestic or Cross-Border?" Bruegel, blog post, June 21, 2018.

[18] Daniel McDowell and David A. Steinberg, "Systemic Strengths, Domestic Deficiencies: The Renminbi's Future as a Reserve Currency," *Journal of Contemporary China*, Vol. 26, No. 108, 2017; Christopher Balding, "Why China Can't Free the Yuan," *Bloomberg View*, August 17, 2017a; Christopher Balding, "China's Economy Is Too Frail to Force Open," *Bloomberg View*, May 17, 2018.

[19] All of the following investments were announced after sanctions were instituted: Russian Direct Investment Fund, "Russian Direct Investment Fund and Vietnamese State Capital Investment Corporation to Create a $500 Million Russian-Vietnamese Investment Platform," press release, May 16, 2016a; Russian Direct Investment Fund, "NIIF and RDIF to Establish a $1BN Russian Indian Investment Fund," press release, October 15, 2016b; Russian Direct Investment Fund, "RCIF and Tus-Holdings to Create Russia-China Venture Fund," press release, November 7, 2016c; Russian Direct Investment Fund, "RDIF and JBIC Agree Key Terms and Conditions for Russia-Japan Investment Fund," press release, April 27, 2017.

success has been limited so far.[20] Related to this is the potential for the use of blockchain technology, a type of digital ledger, to evade sanctions. Several countries have voiced a desire to develop cryptocurrencies that can be traded electronically outside the U.S. dollar clearing system.[21] U.S. authorities have already taken steps to counteract this.[22]

Implications for the U.S. Air Force and the Future of Warfare

Sanctions have proven to be a useful tool for damaging the economies of targeted countries. Strategic consequences are harder to come by. In the case of recent sanctions on Russia, for example, the IMF estimated that the sanctions and a Russian retaliatory ban on agricultural imports reduced Russian GDP between 1 percent and 1.5 percent in the short term and up to 9 percent in the medium term. But Russia is still in Crimea and Eastern Ukraine. A determined government, especially one with significant control over its population, can weather a variety of economic actions.

There are other cases where sanctions have had strategic effect. These include the Banco Delta Asia sanctions mentioned earlier and multilateral comprehensive financial sanctions against Iran in the period preceding and during the negotiations of the Joint Comprehensive Plan of Action, the Iran nuclear agreement. The case of Iran illustrates potential effects of longer-term sanctions. Even when the United States was participating in the Joint Comprehensive Plan of Action, U.S. sanctions on Iran were hurting its economy. With the United States out of the nuclear agreement, those sanctions have multiplied

[20] Tom McGregor, "China Breakthroughs: New International Payments System Goes into Action," CCTV.com, October 19, 2017.

[21] Yaya Fanusie, "Seeking Sanctions Resistance Through Blockchain Technology," *Forbes*, October 11, 2018.

[22] Financial Crimes Enforcement Network, "Advisory on the Iranian Regime's Illicit and Malign Activities and Attempts to Exploit the Financial System," FinCEN Advisory FIN-2018-A006, October 11, 2018.

and, combined with the Iranian government's own economic mismanagement, could lead to further unrest in the country.

Such actions are less likely to have a strategic effect against a great power, especially when core national interests are at stake. North Korea is a tiny economy, and Iran is a midsize one; both have poor economic policies. Sanctions could serve as useful coercive tools against these smaller adversaries. But even if the United States were to retain its centrality in the global economy, sanctions likely would not be a useful substitute for military action against Russia and China; against China, especially, sanctions would be likely to have negative consequences for the United States and Europe because of the complex trading networks that have developed. Instead, economic actions would serve as an adjunct to other instruments of power.

If the power of U.S. sanctions were to decline, they would become less useful as an instrument of coercion or as a substitute for military action. In that case, especially dealing with midlevel and smaller powers, U.S. policymakers might find nonmilitary actions to be more constrained and so lean more toward military intervention than they have in the past, heightening the risk of war. However, they also might choose to become less interventionist. This could lead to less conflict, or it could mean leaving problems to mount in a way that makes conflict more likely.

DoD and USAF have a potential role in maintaining the ability of the United States to gain international support for sanctions. Nations with close military relationships might be more likely to persuade national leaders of the value of supporting the United States in sanctions regimes. Enhancing military relationships with allies through USAF contacts could help influence governments to forge cooperative relationships in fields beyond defense.

CHAPTER EIGHT

Conclusion

Although economic developments, trends, and disputes have generally not been explicit causes of war, they create an environment in which war might be more or less likely and can affect the ability of armed forces to conduct war. The preceding review of six economic trends indicates concerns, especially when those trends are compared with other periods since the end of the Cold War.

U.S. economic power, especially combined with that of allies, will remain dominant, continuing to make the United States an attractive power, but likely will be relatively smaller. This relative decline of U.S. economic power might not directly increase the risk of war but could affect the use of the economic instruments of power, such as sanctions, constraining national security decisionmakers' choices when confronting international problems. Other sources of risk stem from rising barriers and threats to the global trading system, and from both the relative and absolute rise of China (the economy of which is predicted to grow more rapidly than the U.S. economy) as it strives to protect its perceived interests and expand its power. The need for resources that serve as inputs into technology industries also raises uncertainty. Finally, defense industries might not be able to surge production as they have in past major conflicts.

Nonetheless, we judge that the effect of these trends on increasing the risk of war and of U.S. vulnerability is small, and that noticeable war risk will be driven by other trends. Given that overall impression, the next section discusses how the six economic trends are likely to affect war in the future.

Findings

These economic trends could have an effect on who will fight future wars, as well as how, where, when, and why those wars will be fought (Table 8.1). Many of these trends increase the risk of great-power war, although as noted, that increase is small. Only great powers have the ability to raise global trade barriers in a meaningful way, and only other great powers are likely to challenge those that do so. If the rise of China threatens to upend the global system, the United States and Japan are most likely to be affected and have the power to take action. The United States has led the creation of the global system; both the United States and Japan are major beneficiaries of, participants in, and influencers of that system; and both have the military capability and likely the willingness to act should military action be required. Europe has many of those economic characteristics, but its willingness to act is uncertain.

Not all of these trends affect great powers. Resource wars generally occur in developing countries, as either interstate wars or civil wars. Likewise, any decline in U.S. power might spur challenges by midsize adversaries.

While most of these economic trends are unlikely to affect how wars are fought, the shrinking DIB is a notable exception. Trends in the DIB might encourage belligerents to strive for a knockout blow. This would not be unheard of in history—Japan relied on surprise strikes in both the Russo-Japanese war and World War II.

All of these economic trends operate slowly. Accordingly, it appears unlikely that they will be related to war any time before 2020, with risk rising in the latter part of the 2020s. Should war come as a result of economic trends, the reasons will stem largely from fears of global changes that erode a country's growth prospects. This suggests that attempting to force fundamental changes in a country's economic system raises the risk of war. Economic trends also could lead to war as a result of miscalculation—an attack either to take advantage of perceived strength or to act before strength declines.

Regardless of cause, location, timing, and reason, any great-power war is likely to cause enormous economic damage.[1] That reality is one of the underpinnings of the idea—or hope—that current and continued levels of interdependence will serve as a moderating influence on tendencies toward belligerence, whether caused by economic trends or other factors.

Dealing with Uncertainty

This report has focused on trends, but the future rarely develops along a straight line. Therefore, it is worthwhile to consider uncertainties. There are many unexpected events that could knock economic trends off their current path, such as the following:

- The breakdown of the world trading system, the rise of protectionism, and currency devaluations to gain a trading edge all could lead to war as countries try to maintain open markets to stave off economic decline.[2]
- The Chinese economy could implode, leading to a turn toward aggressive nationalism.
- Monopolization of resources essential to economic production also could lead to war.
- Creation of alternative payments systems could lead to the ineffectiveness of U.S. financial sanctions.
- An accelerated economic decline of U.S. allies and a subsequent decision to further lower military spending or to leave their alliance with the United States entirely would substantially alter the balance of power.

Alternatively, there could be positive surprises, such as

---

[1] Reuven Glick and Alan M. Taylor, "Collateral Damage: Trade Disruption and the Economic Impact of War," *The Review of Economics and Statistics*, Vol. 92, No. 1, February 2010.

[2] This was the global pattern before World War II. Harold James, *The End of Globalization: Lessons from the Great Depression*, Cambridge, Mass.: Harvard University Press, 2002.

Table 8.1
Summary of Findings

Trend	Who Will Fight	How the United States Will Fight	Where the United States Will Fight	When the United States Will Fight	Why the United States Will Fight	Other Implications
Increasing pressure on the global trading system	China, United States	No effect	Asia-Pacific, with possible worldwide spillovers	2020s	Fear of economic damage from closing markets	Unlikely overall because mediating institutions can provide alternative dispute resolution
Relative declines in U.S. and allied economic might	Raises risk of challenge by Russia, China, Iran	No effect	No effect	If economic balance makes a difference, likely later 2020s	Miscalculation or opportunistic action to take advantage of perceived weakness	
The rise of China	China, United States, Japan	No effect	Asia-Pacific, with possible worldwide spillovers	Uncertain	Miscalculation; a rising China will see an opportunity to take something it wants; the United States will step in to halt China's rise; or a China in crisis will go to war to spur cohesion and nationalism	Long-term damage to the global economy

Table 8.1—Continued

Trend	Who Will Fight	How the United States Will Fight	Where the United States Will Fight	When the United States Will Fight	Why the United States Will Fight	Other Implications
The search for new resources	Smaller countries	Interventions in small wars and civil wars	Developing countries	Uncertain	To protect a partner under attack or to forestall monopolization of a resource	Unlikely because of robust markets, substitution, and technological change
The shrinking defense industrial base	No effect	Readiness and resilience negatively affected so war duration might lengthen or temptation to use more-powerful weapons or deliver knockout blow might rise	Uncertain	Might lessen the frequency of war	No effect	Negative labor force trends could encourage more investment in skills and training; advanced manufacturing processes could mitigate negative labor-force trends
Decreasing power of U.S. sanctions	Raises risk of United States considering military action	No effect, although resort to war might be quicker	No effect	If sanctions substitute for war, sooner than otherwise	No effect	Even if U.S. leverage declines, multilateral leverage of United States and allies likely will stay strong

- technological advances that increase economic growth in the advanced economies and provide a warfighting edge for the United States and its alliance partners
- discovery of new resource deposits in allied and friendly countries.

The problem with all of these is that, in the language of probability and statistics, they are all point estimates in an infinite range of possibilities. It is impossible to predict all—or even the most likely—surprises, which means it is also impossible to plan for them.

An alternative, however, would be to take measures that will enable the nation to maintain military preparedness, warfighting capabilities, and national security in the face of surprises.[3] Among these measures are two concrete steps that the United States can take.

The first is to repair and strengthen the U.S. economy, especially its government budget. The CBO projects that the 2018 federal deficit will be 3.9 percent of GDP, the smallest deficit projected through 2048.[4] The rise of the deficit will cause the rise of federal debt held by the public, projected to be 78 percent of GDP in 2018 and 99 percent in 2030, the highest level since 1946, when it hit 106 percent in the wake of borrowing to fund World War II. Between 1960 and 2008, it ranged between 20 percent and 50 percent.

The CBO has been warning about the rise of debt in similar language every year since 2011, when the debt was 66 percent of GDP:

> When outstanding debt is relatively small, the federal government is able to borrow money at lower rates to cover unexpected costs, such as those that arise from recessions, financial crises, natural disasters, or wars. By contrast, when outstanding debt is large, the government has less flexibility to address financial and economic crises. A large debt also can compromise a country's national security by constraining military spending in times of

---

[3] The idea of taking steps to remain relatively unaffected or even to emerge stronger in the face of negative surprises is explored at length in Nassim Nicholas Taleb, *The Black Swan: The Impact of the Highly Improbable*, New York: Random House, 2007; and Nassim Nicholas Taleb, *Antifragile: Things That Gain from Disorder*, New York: Random House, 2012.

[4] CBO, *The 2018 Long-Term Budget Outlook*, Washington, D.C., June 2018b.

international crisis or by limiting the government's ability to prepare for (or respond to) such a crisis.[5]

Accordingly, it would be useful for the government to get control of its finances. However, given past performance, DoD and USAF can benefit by planning for a financially constrained spending environment on the expectation that the public will be unlikely to support large defense budgets when popular entitlement programs are at risk of being cut.[6]

Controlling spending on entitlement programs will be one key to controlling federal spending and debt. In addition to contingency planning, USAF leaders can stress that DoD has already undergone significant entitlement reform. The Blended Retirement System changes the retirement benefits of every airman joining USAF after January 1, 2018; some serving airmen also can join. This new system is expected to save significant taxpayer money.[7] Because DoD has already started entitlement reform, it can serve as an example for the rest of the government in considering entitlement reform to help achieve fiscal stability, reduce deficits, and improve U.S. national security.

The second step the United States could take is to strengthen global institutional structures that the United States created and still dominates with allies.[8] In fact, the security policy of the United States is to work in concert with allies and partners, and global institutions provide an efficient way to do that. While calling on allies and partners to increase their contributions to security, the United States also rec-

---

5 CBO, 2018b, p. 9.

6 Howard Shatz, "The Long-Term Budget Shortfall and National Security: A Problem the United States Should Stop Avoiding," *War on the Rocks*, November 6, 2017.

7 For one analysis of the Blended Retirement System, see Beth J. Asch, Michael G. Mattock, and James Hosek, *The Blended Retirement System: Retention Effects and Continuation Pay Cost Estimates for the Armed Services*, Santa Monica, Calif.: RAND Corporation, RR-1887-OSD, 2017.

8 Howard J. Shatz and David A. Shlapak, "The Made-in-America Global Security and Economic System Still Serves U.S. Interests," *Plain Dealer*, October 19, 2016.

ognized "the invaluable advantages that our strong relationships with allies and partners deliver."[9]

Even with the growth of China and the relative decline of Europe and Japan, the United States and its allies combined will be the dominant economies through 2030. Even with more-limited U.S. production of fourth- and fifth-generation fighter jets, the United States and its allies will produce a variety of fighters and perhaps find redundancy and resilience through that variety. As the largest importers, the United States and its allies can retain their ability to take the lead in shaping global economic standards. Although the institutional arrangements founded at the end of World War II might need reform, the reasons for founding them remain—the need for venues to mediate disputes, agreeing to common rules, and generally pursuing joint efforts to pursue beneficial development where joint efforts are useful—and those reasons are sure to last through 2030.

---

9 White House, 2017b, p. 2.

APPENDIX

Key Production Lines of Fourth- and Fifth-Generation Fighter Aircraft

Table A.1 details the world's current major fourth- and fifth-generation fighter aircraft programs by prime contractor and production line status.

Table A.1
Production Status and Forecast of Major Fourth- and Fifth-Generation Fighter Aircraft Platforms by Prime Contractors

Country	Model	Generation	Prime Contractor	Currently in Production	Year of First Delivery	Production Status and Forecast
United States	F-35 A/B/C	5th	Lockheed Martin	Yes	2011	Some 2,200 new U.S. deliveries and 650 export deliveries expected through 2030s
United States	F-22	5th	Lockheed Martin	No	2005	No future deliveries; production line closed in 2012
United States	F/A-18E/F	4th	Boeing	Yes	1996	Some 110 new U.S. and 28 export deliveries contracted through 2020s; additional export deliveries possible
United States	F-15	4th	Boeing	Yes	1972	No new U.S. deliveries expected; 36 new export deliveries planned through 2020s; more are possible
United States	F-16	4th	Lockheed Martin	Yes	1978	No new U.S. deliveries expected; 16 new export deliveries planned through 2020s; some 100–200 more possible if pending deal with India approved
UK, Germany Italy, Spain	Eurofighter Typhoon	4th	Airbus, BAE Systems, Leonardo-Finmeccanica	Yes	2003	Production line closure originally planned for 2020, but recently extended through 2023 by Kuwaiti order of 28 aircraft; future export orders unlikely due to competitor unit price; no new European acquisitions planned

Table A.1—Continued

Country	Model	Generation	Prime Contractor	Currently in Production	Year of First Delivery	Production Status and Forecast
France	Rafale	4th	Dassault Aviation	Yes	2000	Some 100–300 export deliveries are planned to India, Qatar, and Egypt over next decade; Malaysia, Singapore, and UAE also possible export clients; no deliveries are planned to France in 2019–2020; 28 fourth-tranche deliveries to France set to begin in 2021; 45 fifth-tranche deliveries to France possible in out-years
France	Mirage 2000	4th	Dassault Aviation	No	1983	Production line closed in 2007
Sweden	JAS-39 Gripen	4th	Saab	Yes	1993	Some 60–80 new deliveries to Sweden and at least 36 export deliveries to Brazil planned through the 2020s; candidate for multiple other export opportunities due to low operating costs vs. capabilities including in Eastern and Central Europe, India, Botswana, Canada, Indonesia, and the Philippines
Russia	Su-35	4th	Sukhoi	Yes	2012	Production originally planned to end in mid-2020s, but likely will be extended due to delays in development of fifth-generation Su-57; 130 new deliveries planned to Russian government through 2027; 11 future export deliveries also scheduled to Indonesia; new export orders to other states are likely, including possibly to China, UAE, and India, though none are on the books currently

Table A.1—Continued

Country	Model	Generation	Prime Contractor	Currently in Production	Year of First Delivery	Production Status and Forecast
Russia	MiG-35	4th	Mikoyan	Yes	2018?	70–170 new deliveries to Russian government expected for the next decade as development of fifth-generation Su-57 continues. Future export deliveries likely but none currently scheduled.
Russia, India[a]	Su-57	5th	Sukhoi	No	2022	Fifth-generation fighter still in development; India withdrew in 2018 from decade-long joint venture of fifth-generation fighter aircraft; first delivery expected in 2022; 60–70 new deliveries to Russia planned through 2027; platform intended for domestic demand; no exports expected in foreseeable future
Russia	Su-30	4th	Sukhoi	Yes	1992	Russia expected to procure 66 new Su-30s between 2018 and 2022; future export units include six to Myanmar, 24 to Kazakhstan, 12 to Belarus, and 8–12 to Bangladesh; possible future export deals have also been rumored involving Iran, Venezuela, and Armenia

Table A.1—Continued

Country	Model	Generation	Prime Contractor	Currently in Production	Year of First Delivery	Production Status and Forecast
Russia	Su-34	4th	Sukhoi	Yes	2006	Russia expected to sign a contract to procure 90–100 new Su-34s in next couple years, but acquisition orders apparently not completed; Algeria, Jordan, China, and various Central Asian countries rumored as potential export markets, but no contracts appear completed (Note: Su-32 is the export version of the Su-34)
Russia	Su-27	4th	Sukhoi	Yes	1985	Production of Su-27 expected to draw to a close soon, having been replaced by numerous Su-30 variants
Russia	MiG-29	4th	Mikoyan	Yes	1982	Production of Su-27 expected to draw to a close soon, having been replaced by MiG-35 variants
China	J-20	5th	Chengdu Aircraft Corp	Yes	2017	Platform intended for domestic demand; no exports expected in foreseeable future; production demand unknown
China	J-10	4th	Chengdu Aircraft Corp	Yes	2006?	Production demand unknown
China	J-11	4th	Shenyang Aircraft Corp	Yes	1998?	Production demand unknown
China	J-15	4th	Shenyang Aircraft Corp	Yes	2015?	Production demand unknown

Table A.1—Continued

Country	Model	Generation	Prime Contractor	Currently in Production	Year of First Delivery	Production Status and Forecast
China	J-16	4th	Shenyang Aircraft Corp	Yes	2016?	Production demand unknown
China	J-31	4th	Shenyang Aircraft Corp	No	2020?	Possibly in development; production demand unknown
China, Pakistan	JF-17	4th	Chengdu Aircraft Corp, Pakistan Aeronautical Complex	Yes	2007?	Production demand unknown
South Korea, Indonesia	KF-X	5th	Korean Aerospace Industries, Indonesian Aerospace	No	2027	Joint South Korean–Indonesian fifth-generation fighter still in development; production expected to begin in 2027; no exports expected in foreseeable future
Turkey, UK	TF-X	5th	Turkish Aerospace Industries, BAE Systems	No	2030	Joint British-Turkish fifth-generation fighter still in development; production expected to begin in 2030; platform intended for domestic demand; no exports expected in foreseeable future
Japan	F-3	5th	Mitsubishi	No	2031	Japanese fifth-generation fighter still in development; production expected to begin in 2031; platform intended for domestic demand; no exports expected in foreseeable future

Table A.1—Continued

Country	Model	Generation	Prime Contractor	Currently in Production	Year of First Delivery	Production Status and Forecast
India	AMCA	5th	Hindustan Aeronautics Limited	No	2027	Indian fifth-generation fighter still in development; production expected to begin in 2027; no exports expected in foreseeable future

SOURCES: IHS Jane's, "Equipment Explorer," online database, undated; Defense Industry Daily, "Defense Program Tracker," subscription-only database, undated; Victor Litovkin, "Three Aircraft in One," *Russia Beyond*, March 8, 2012; Dave Majumdar, "The JAS-39 Gripen: Sweden's Cheap (and Deadly) Fighter Plane," *The National Interest*, September 24, 2015; Giovanni de Briganti, "Eurofighter Partners Face Hard Decisions on Production, Damages As Orders Run Out," Defense-Aerospace.com, October 10, 2016; Franz-Stefan Gady, "Iran, Russia Inching Closer to Su-30 Fighter Jet Deal," *The Diplomat*, December 1, 2016; Bernardi et al., 2017; Pierre Tran, "Dassault Credits Rafale Export Deals as Financial Savior," *Defense News*, March 8, 2017; Reuben Johnson, "Russia to Ramp-Up Production of Sukhoi Su-34," AINonline.com, April 10, 2017; Tony Osborne, "Typhoon Production Nudges to 2023," ShowNews, June 18, 2017; "Russia May Start Exporting Advanced MiG-35 Fighter Jet in Couple of Years," TASS Russian News Agency, June 19, 2017; "Russia to Reschedule Su-30SM Fighter Delivery to Belarus over Technical Changes," DefenseWorld.net, July 18, 2017; Valerie Insinna, "Despite Obstacles, Saab Still Hopeful for Future Gripen C Sales," *Defense News*, November 12, 2017b; Office of the Secretary of Defense, 2018; Dmitry Gorenburg, "Russian Air Force Procurement Plans," *Russian Military Reform*, January 24, 2018; "More Russian Su-35 Fighters Rumored to Join PLAAF," *Asia Times*, March 9, 2018; "Kazakhstan to Acquire Additional Su-30SM Fighters from Russia," Defense-Aerospace.com, March 11, 2018; "Key Facts About Russia's Su-30 Multirole Fighter Jet," TASS Russian News Agency, May 3, 2018; Beth Stevenson, "Gripen Production Line Established in Brazil," IHS Jane's Defence Industry, May 10, 2018.

[a] India withdrew from the fifth-generation fighter aircraft program in April 2018. Data in this table are current as of mid-2018.

References

Abbot, Evelyn, *A History of Greece, Part III: From the Thirty Years' Peace to the Fall of the Thirty at Athens, 445–403 B.C.*, London and Bombay: Longmans, Green and Co., 1900.

Abi-Habib, Maria, "How China Got Sri Lanka to Cough Up a Port," *New York Times*, June 25, 2018.

Aerospace Industries Association, *Fostering the Manufacturing & Defense Industrial Base of the Future*, Arlington, Va., April 2018.

Allison, Graham, "The Thucydides Trap: Are the U.S. and China Headed for War?" *The Atlantic*, September 24, 2015. As of August 29, 2018: https://www.theatlantic.com/international/archive/2015/09/united-states-china-war-thucydides-trap/406756/

———, *Destined for War? Can America and China Escape Thucydides's Trap?* New York, Houghton Mifflin Harcourt Publishing Company, 2017a.

———, "How Trump and Xi Could Stumble into War," *Washington Post*, March 31, 2017b.

———, "War Between China and the United States Isn't Inevitable, but It's Likely: An Excerpt from Graham Allison's *Destined for War*," *National Post*, March 5, 2018. As of August 29, 2018: https://nationalpost.com/opinion/war-between-china-and-the-united-states-isnt-inevitable-but-its-likely-an-excerpt-from-graham-allisons-destined-for-war

Anderton, Charles, "Economic Theorizing of Conflict: Historical Contributions, Future Possibilities," *Defence and Peace Economics*, Vol. 14, No. 3, 2003, pp. 209–222.

Arena, Mark, John Graser, and Paul DeLuca, *Implications of an Air Force Budget Downturn on the Aircraft Industrial Base: An Exploratory Analysis*, Santa Monica, Calif.: RAND Corporation, RR-248-AF, 2013. As of March 2, 2019: https://www.rand.org/pubs/research_reports/RR248.html

Asch, Beth J., Michael G. Mattock, and James Hosek, *The Blended Retirement System: Retention Effects and Continuation Pay Cost Estimates for the Armed Services*, Santa Monica, Calif.: RAND Corporation, RR-1887-OSD, 2017. As of December 20, 2018:
https://www.rand.org/pubs/research_reports/RR1887.html

Asian Infrastructure Investment Bank, "Partnerships," webpage, 2018. As of December 17, 2018:
https://www.aiib.org/en/about-aiib/who-we-are/partnership/index.html

"Backgrounder: The AIIB," *Xinhua*, January 16, 2016.

Bagli, Charles, "Two Giants Join a Merger Parade in Arms Industry," *New York Times*, July 4, 1997.

Balding, Christopher, "Why China Can't Free the Yuan," *Bloomberg View*, August 17, 2017a. As of July 4, 2018:
https://www.bloomberg.com/view/articles/2017-08-18/why-china-can-t-free-the-yuan

———, "China Bets on More State Control for 2018," Bloomberg, December 26, 2017b. As of December 24, 2018:
https://www.bloomberg.com/opinion/articles/2017-12-26/china-bets-on-more-state-control-for-2018

———, "China's Economy Is Too Frail to Force Open," *Bloomberg View*, May 17, 2018. As of July 4, 2018:
https://www.bloomberg.com/view/articles/2018-05-18/china-s-economy-is-too-frail-to-force-open

Balis, Christina, and Henrik Heidenkamp, *Prospects for the European Defence Industrial Base*, RUSI Occasional Paper, September 9, 2014.

Barone, Barbara, and Robert Bendini, *Protectionism in the G20 (2015)*, Policy Department, General-Directorate for External Policies, European Parliament, DG EXPO/B/PolDep/Note/2015_136, March 2015.

Beckley, Michael, "Economic Development and Military Effectiveness," *Journal of Strategic Studies*, Vol. 33, No. 1, February 2010, pp. 43–79.

Bell, Dylan, Jeffrey Fallat, Gregory Sterley, and Ehssan Alsuhibani, *The Future of Additive Manufacturing in the U.S. Military*, Maxwell Air Force Base, Ala.: Air War College, Air University, March 17, 2017.

Bernardi, Beatrice, John Sneller, Charles Hollosi, Ben Moores, and Mark Bobbi, "Fight-Gen vs. Fourth-Gen: Technology Meets Platform Maturity in a Competing Fighter Market," Jane's Defence Industry & Markets Intelligence Center, October 26, 2017.

Birkler, John, Paul Bracken, Gordon T. Lee, Mark A. Lorell, Soumen Saha, and Shane Tierney, *Keeping a Competitive U.S. Military Aircraft Market Aloft: Findings from an Analysis of the Industrial Base*, Santa Monica, Calif.: RAND Corporation, MG-1133-OSD, 2011. As of March 2, 2019: https://www.rand.org/pubs/monographs/MG1133.html

Birkler, John, Joseph P. Large, Giles K. Smith, and Fred Timson, *Reconstituting a Production Capability: Past Experience, Restart Criteria and Suggested Policies*, Santa Monica, Calif.: RAND Corporation, MR-273-ACQ, 1993. As of October 18, 2018: https://www.rand.org/pubs/monograph_reports/MR273.html

Blattman, Christopher, and Edward Miguel, "Civil War," *Journal of Economic Literature*, Vol. 48, No. 1, March 2010, pp. 3–57.

Boeing, "Back to the Future: Boeing Delivers the First Super Hornet to the Navy in Two Years," press release, February 20, 2018a.

———, "A Super Hornet Returns to Its Nest: The Boeing Service Life Modification Program Begins," press release, May 7, 2018b.

Bolkcom, Christopher, and Ellen Schwarzler, *Russian Fighter Aircraft Industrial Base: Parallels with the United States?* Washington, D.C.: Congressional Research Service, RL30730, April 9, 2002.

Bradsher, Keith, "Amid Tension, China Blocks Vital Exports to Japan," *New York Times*, September 22, 2010.

Brochmann, Marit, and Nils Petter Gleditsch, "Shared Rivers and Conflict—A Reconsideration," *Political Geography*, Vol. 31, No. 8, November 2012, pp. 519–527.

Brown, Chad P., and Douglas A. Irwin, *The GATT's Starting Point: Tariff Levels Circa 1947*, Cambridge, Mass.: National Bureau of Economic Research, NBER Working Paper 21782, December 2015.

Browne, Andrew, "The Underclass That Threatens Xi's 'China Dream,'" *Wall Street Journal*, December 5, 2017.

Buterbaugh, Kevin, and Richard Fulton, *The WTO Primer: Tracing Trade's Visible Hand Through Case Studies*, New York: Palgrave MacMillan, 2007.

Callen, Tim, "PPP Versus the Market: Which Weight Matters?" *Finance & Development*, Vol. 44, No. 1, March 2007. As of December 20, 2018: https://www.imf.org/external/pubs/ft/fandd/2007/03/basics.htm

Campbell, Thomas, Christopher Williams, Olga Ivanova, and Banning Garrett, *Could 3D Printing Change the World? Technologies, Potential, and Implications of Additive Manufacturing*, Washington, D.C.: Atlantic Council, Strategic Foresight Report, October 2011.

Caselli, Francesco, Massimo Morelli, and Dominic Rohner, *The Geography of Interstate Resource Wars*, Washington, D.C.: National Bureau of Economic Research, NBER Working Paper No. 18978, April 2013.

Casey, John P., "Testimony of John P. Casey before the Senate Armed Services Committee, Subcommittee on Seapower, 115th Congress, Supporting the 355-Ship Navy with Focus on Submarine Industrial Base," Washington, D.C., May 24, 2017.

CBO—*See* U.S. Congressional Budget Office.

Censer, Marjorie, "Defense Companies Brace for a Different Kind of Consolidation This Time Around," *Washington Post*, January 12, 2014.

Chellany, Brahma, "China Is Stealthily Waging a Water War," *Toronto Globe and Mail*, January 12, 2018. As of July 1, 2018:
https://www.theglobeandmail.com/opinion/china-is-stealthily-waging-a-water-war/article37583969/

Cheng Xiaobo, ed. [程晓波主编], *Big Data Report on Trade Cooperation Under the Belt and Road Initiative* [一带一路贸易合作大数据报告], Belt and Road Big Data Center of the State Information Center [国家信息中心"一带一路"大数据中心] and SINOIMEX [大连瀚闻资讯有限公司], May 2018.

China Institute of International Studies, *China's Diplomatic Efforts to Promote Energy and Resources Cooperation Along the "One Belt and One Road,"* Beijing, CIIS Report No. 5, May 2015.

Cohen, Raphael S., Nathan Chandler, Shira Efron, Bryan Frederick, Eugeniu Han, Kurt Klein, Forrest Morgan, Ashley L. Rhoades, Howard J. Shatz, and Yuliya Shokh, *The Future of Warfare in 2030: Project Overview and Conclusions*, Santa Monica, Calif.: RAND Corporation, RR-2849/1-AF, 2020. As of May 2020:
https://www.rand.org/pubs/research_reports/RR2849z1.html

Cohen, Raphael S., Eugeniu Han, and Ashley L. Rhoades, *Geopolitical Trends and the Future of Warfare: The Changing Global Environment and Its Implications for the U.S. Air Force*, Santa Monica, Calif.: RAND Corporation, RR-2849/2-AF, 2020. As of May 2020:
https://www.rand.org/pubs/research_reports/RR2849z2.html

Colgan, Jeff D., "Fueling the Fire: Pathways from Oil to War," *International Security*, Vol. 38, No. 2, Fall 2013, pp. 147–180.

Collier, Irwin L., *The Estimation of Gross Domestic Product and Its Growth Rate for the German Democratic Republic*, Washington, D.C.: World Bank, Staff Working Papers Number 773, November 1985.

Connolly, Richard, and Mathieu Boulegue, *Russia's New State Armament Programme: Implications for the Russian Armed Forces and Military Capabilities to 2027*, London: Chatham House, research paper, May 2018.

Cuccias, Brian, "Statement of Brian Cuccias, President, Ingalls Shipbuilding, Huntington Ingalls Industries, Subcommittee on Seapower, Senate Armed Services Committee, 115th Congress," Washington, D.C., May 24, 2017.

de Briganti, Giovanni, "Eurofighter Partners Face Hard Decisions on Production, Damages As Orders Run Out," Defense-Aerospace.com, October 10, 2016.

Defense Industry Daily, "Defense Program Tracker," subscription-only database, undated.

Defense Logistics Agency Strategic Materials, "Our Offices," webpage, undated. As of May 28, 2019:
https://www.dla.mil/HQ/Acquisition/StrategicMaterials/About/OurOffices/

———, "Annual Materials Plan for FY 2019," [Potential Disposals], DLA-SM-18-3151, October 3, 2018a. As of May 28, 2019:
https://www.dla.mil/Portals/104/Documents/StrategicMaterials/Announcements/3151%20FY19%20AMP.pdf?ver=2018-10-03-091746-287

———, "Annual Materials Plan for FY 2019," [Acquisitions], DLA-SM-18-3152, October 3, 2018b. As of May 28, 2019:
https://www.dla.mil/Portals/104/Documents/StrategicMaterials/Announcements/3152%20FY19%20AMP_ACQ.pdf?ver=2018-10-03-091748-770

Deign, Jason, "Reliance on Congo Cobalt Grows Despite European Discoveries," GTM: Greentech Media, June 5, 2018. As of July 24, 2018:
https://www.greentechmedia.com/articles/read/congo-cobalt-reliance-grows-despite-europe-discoveries#gs.wEts2GE

Deloitte and Manufacturing Institute, *The Skills Gap in U.S. Manufacturing: 2015 and Beyond*, New York, 2015.

Desai, Pratima, "Battery Chemical Surplus Sparks Plunge in Cobalt Price," Reuters, July 31, 2018. As of August 27, 2018:
https://www.reuters.com/article/us-cobalt-chemicals-prices/battery-chemical-surplus-sparks-plunge-in-cobalt-price-idUSKBN1KL1OT

Dobbins, James, Andrew Scobell, Edmund J. Burke, David C. Gompert, Derek Grossman, Eric Heginbotham, and Howard J. Shatz, *Conflict with China Revisited: Prospects, Consequences, and Strategies for Deterrence*, Santa Monica, Calif.: RAND Corporation, PE-248-A, 2017. As of June 29, 2018:
https://www.rand.org/pubs/perspectives/PE248.html

Dobbins, James, Howard J. Shatz, and Suhail Ali Wyne, *Russia Is a Rogue, Not a Peer; China Is a Peer, Not a Rogue: Different Challenges, Different Responses*, Santa Monica, Calif.: RAND Corporation, PE-310-A, 2019. As of March 2, 2019:
https://www.rand.org/pubs/perspectives/PE310.html

Dollar, David, *China's Rebalancing: Lessons from East Asian Economic History*, Washington, D.C.: Brookings Institution, John L. Thornton China Center Working Paper Series, October 2013.

Donnan, Shawn, "Trade Talks Lead to 'Death of Doha and Birth of New WTO," *Financial Times*, December 20, 2015. As of June 18, 2018:
https://www.ft.com/content/97e8525e-a740-11e5-9700-2b669a5aeb83

Duijm, Patty, and Dirk Schoenmaker, "European Bank Mergers: Domestic or Cross-Border?" Bruegel, blog post, June 21, 2018. As of July 4, 2018:
http://bruegel.org/2018/06/european-bank-mergers-domestic-or-cross-border/

Eaglen, Mackenzie M., and Eric Sayers, *Maintaining the Superiority of America's Defense Industrial Base*, Washington, D.C.: Heritage Foundation, Backgrounder No. 2276, May 22, 2009.

Efron, Shira, Kurt Klein, and Raphael S. Cohen, *Environment, Geography and the Future of Warfare: The Changing Global Environment and Its Implications for the U.S. Air Force*, Santa Monica, Calif.: RAND Corporation, RR-2849/5-AF, 2020. As of May 2020:
https://www.rand.org/pubs/research_reports/RR2849z5.html

Engelhardt, Joseph P., *Desert Shield and Desert Storm: A Chronology and Troop List for the 1990–1991 Persian Gulf Crisis*, Carlisle, Pa.: Strategic Studies Institute, U.S. Army War College, SSI Special Report AD-A234 743, March 25, 1991.

European Chamber, *China Manufacturing 2025: Putting Industrial Policy Ahead of Market Forces*, Beijing, 2017.

European Commission, *EU-China—A Strategic Outlook*, Joint Communication to the European Parliament, the European Council and the Council, Strasbourg: JOIN(2019) 5 final, March 12, 2019. As of May 30, 2019:
https://ec.europa.eu/commission/publications/eu-china-strategic-outlook-commission-contribution-european-council-21-22-march-2019_en

Evenett, Simon J., and Johannes Fritz, *Going Spare: Steel, Excess Capacity, and Protectionism*, London: CEPR Press, 22nd Global Trade Alert Report, 2018a.

———, *The Global Trade Alert Database Handbook*, St. Gallen, Switzerland, March 28, 2018b.

"F-16 Jet Production in India Will Be Exclusive: Lockheed," *Times of India*, March 19, 2018.

Fanusie, Yaya, "Seeking Sanctions Resistance Through Blockchain Technology," *Forbes*, October 11, 2018. As of December 24, 2018:
https://www.forbes.com/sites/yayafanusie/2018/10/11/seeking-sanctions-resistance-through-blockchain-technology/#13c1b9396392

Federal Reserve Bank of St. Louis, "Germany/U.S. Foreign Exchange Rate (DISCONTINUED) [EXGEUS]," undated. As of December 18, 2018:
https://fred.stlouisfed.org/series/EXGEUS

Fei, John, "China's Overseas Military Base in Djibouti: Features, Motivations, and Policy Implications," *China Brief*, Vol. 17, Issue 17, December 22, 2017. As of July 24, 2018:
https://jamestown.org/program/chinas-overseas-military-base-djibouti-features-motivations-policy-implications/

Fewsmith, Joseph, "China and the WTO: The Politics Behind the Agreement," National Bureau of Asian Research, November 1999. As of June 28, 2018:
https://www.iatp.org/files/China_and_the_WTO_The_Politics_Behind_the_Agre.htm

Financial Crimes Enforcement Network, "Advisory on the Iranian Regime's Illicit and Malign Activities and Attempts to Exploit the Financial System," FinCEN Advisory FIN-2018-A006, October 11, 2018. As of December 24, 2018:
https://www.fincen.gov/sites/default/files/advisory/2018-10-11/Iran%20Advisory%20FINAL%20508.pdf

Fischer, Dietrich, and Jurgen Brauer, "Twenty Questions for Peace Economics: A Research Agenda," *Defence and Peace Economics*, Vol. 14, No. 3, 2003, pp. 223–236.

Fitch Ratings, "China's One Belt, One Road Initiative Brings Risks," press release, January 25, 2017.

Forest, Benjamin D., *The Future of Additive Manufacturing in Air Force Acquisition*, Maxwell Air Force Base, Ala.: Air War College, Air University, March 22, 2017.

Frater, Patrick, "'Wolf Warrior II's' Massive Success Forces Studios to Rethink China Approach," *Variety*, August 31, 2017. As of July 24, 2018:
https://variety.com/2017/biz/news/china-wolf-warrior-ii-1202543266/

Frederick, Bryan, and Nathan Chandler, *Restraint and the Future of Warfare: The Changing Global Environment and Its Implications for the U.S. Air Force*, Santa Monica, Calif.: RAND Corporation, RR-2849/6-AF, 2020. As of May 2020:
https://www.rand.org/pubs/research_reports/RR2849z6.html

Freedberg, Sydney J., Jr., "US Defense Budget Not That Much Bigger Than China, Russia: Gen. Milley," *Breaking Defense*, May 22, 2018. As of July 5, 2018:
https://breakingdefense.com/2018/05/us-defense-budget-not-that-much-bigger-than-china-russia-gen-milley/

Freedman, Lawrence, and Efraim Karsh, *The Gulf Conflict 1990–1991: Diplomacy and War in the New World Order*, Princeton, N.J.: Princeton University Press, 1993.

The Future of European Defence: Tackling the Productivity Challenge, New York: McKinsey and Company, 2013.

Gady, Franz-Stefan, "Iran, Russia Inching Closer to Su-30 Fighter Jet Deal," *The Diplomat*, December 1, 2016.

Galbraith, James K., Corwin Priest, and George Purcell, "Economic Equality and Victory in War: An Empirical Investigation," *Defence and Peace Economics*, Vol. 18, No. 5, 2007, pp. 431–449.

Gallagher, Mike, "Hedging Our Bets: Reviving Defense Industrial Surge Capacity," *War on the Rocks*, December 1, 2017.

Garfinkel, Michelle R., and Stergios Skaperdas, "Economics of Conflict: An Overview," in Todd Sandler and Keith Hartley, eds., *Handbook of Defense Economics*, Vol. 2, Amsterdam: Elsevier B.V., 2007, Chapter 22, pp. 649–709.

"Germany Urges EU to Fight Back Against Russia Sanctions Bill," Radio Free Europe/Radio Liberty, August 1, 2017.

Glick, Reuven, and Alan M. Taylor, "Collateral Damage: Trade Disruption and the Economic Impact of War," *The Review of Economics and Statistics*, Vol. 92, No. 1, February 2010, pp. 102–127.

Global Trade Alert, "Interventions Per Year," online spreadsheet, undated. As of December 20, 2018:
https://www.globaltradealert.org/download/global_dynamics/interventions/

Gorenburg, Dmitry, "Russian Air Force Procurement Plans," *Russian Military Reform*, January 24, 2018. As of July 6, 2018:
https://russiamil.wordpress.com/2018/01/24/russian-air-force-procurement-plans-2/

Gros, Daniel, "Globalisation: The Hype, the Reality, and the Causes of the Recent Slowdown in Global Trade," VOX: CEPR Policy Portal, June 30, 2017. As of June 18, 2018:
https://voxeu.org/article/hype-reality-and-causes-global-trade-slowdown

Group of Seven, "The Charlevoix G7 Summit Communique," Charlevoix, Quebec, June 9, 2018. As of June 18, 2018:
https://g7.gc.ca/en/official-documents/charlevoix-g7-summit-communique/

Guay, Terrence, *The Transatlantic Defense Industrial Base: Restructuring Scenarios and Their Implications*, Carlisle, Pa.: U.S. Army War College, April 2005.

Gutner, Tamar, "AIIB: Is the Chinese-Led Development Bank a Role Model?" Council on Foreign Relations, blog post, June 25, 2018. As of December 17, 2018:
https://www.cfr.org/blog/aiib-chinese-led-development-bank-role-model

Harrison, Mark, "Economic Growth and Slowdown," in Edwin Bacon and Mark Sandle, eds., *Brezhnev Reconsidered*, London and Basingstoke: Palgrave, 2002, pp. 38–67.

———, *The Economics of Conflict and Coercion*, Singapore: World Scientific, 2014.

Heide, Dana, Till Hoppe, Stephan Scheuer, and Klaus Stratmann, "EU Ambassadors Band Together Against Silk Road," Handelsblatt Global, April 17, 2018. As of December 17, 2018:
https://www.handelsblatt.com/today/politics/china-first-eu-ambassadors-band-together-against-silk-road/23581860.html?ticket=ST-115677-BJXN07dAHYDBQdssZ7dK-ap1

Heifetz, Stephen, and Evan Sherwood, "Those Other Economic Sanctions: Section 311 Special Measures," *The Banking Law Journal*, Vol. 131, No. 9, September 2014, pp. 688–694.

Hendrix, Cullen S., *Oil Prices and Interstate Conflict Behavior*, Washington, D.C.: Peterson Institute for International Economics, Working Paper 14-3, July 2014.

Hoekman, Bernard, and Aaditya Matoo, *Services Trade Liberalization and Regulatory Reform: Re-Invigorating International Competition*, Washington, D.C.: World Bank, Policy Research Working Paper 5517, January 2011. As of December 24, 2018:
https://openknowledge.worldbank.org/handle/10986/3290

Hofman, Bert, "Reflections on Forty Years of China's Reforms," speech at the Fudan University's Fanhai School of International Finance, January 2018. As of December 17, 2018:
http://pubdocs.worldbank.org/en/934911517472447837/Reflections-on-40-years-of-reforms-final.pdf

Hsu, Sara, "How China's Asian Infrastructure Investment Bank Fared Its First Year," *Forbes*, January 14, 2017. As of December 17, 2018:
https://www.forbes.com/sites/sarahsu/2017/01/14/how-chinas-asian-infrastructure-investment-bank-fared-its-first-year/#3f92b1d65a7f

Hufbauer, Gary Clyde, Jeffrey J. Schott, Kimberly Ann Elliott, and Barbara Oegg, *Economic Sanctions Reconsidered*, 3rd ed., Washington, D.C.: Peterson Institute for International Economics, 2007.

IHS Jane's, "Equipment Explorer," online database, undated.

IMF—*See* International Monetary Fund.

"In Focus: End of F-22 Production Closes Chapter in Eventful History," *Flight International*, April 2, 2012.

Insinna, Valeria, "Fate of A-10, F-15 to Be Decided This Fall," *Defense News*, September 17, 2017a.

———, "Despite Obstacles, Saab Still Hopeful for Future Gripen C Sales," *Defense News*, November 12, 2017b.

———, "Boeing Scores Big with F-15, KC-46 Contracts with Foreign Militaries," *Defense News*, December 22, 2017c.

———, "Boeing and Kuwait Cement Super Hornet Deal," *Defense News*, March 30, 2018.

International Comparison Program, *Purchasing Power Parities and the Real Size of World Economies: A Comprehensive Report of the 2011 International Comparison Program*, Washington, D.C.: World Bank, 2015.

International Energy Agency, *Global EV Outlook 2018: Towards Cross-Modal Electrification*, Paris, 2018.

International Monetary Fund, "IMF Executive Board Approves Major Overhaul of Quotas and Governance," Washington, D.C., Press Release No. 10/418, November 5, 2010.

———, "IMF Launches New SDR Basket Including Chinese Renminbi, Determines New Currency Amounts," Press Release, September 30, 2016. As of June 26, 2018:
https://www.imf.org/en/News/Articles/2016/09/30/AM16-PR16440-IMF-Launches-New-SDR-Basket-Including-Chinese-Renminbi

———, "Russian Federation: Staff Concluding Statement of the 2018 Article IV Mission," Washington, D.C., May 23, 2018a. As of May 24, 2018:
http://www.imf.org/en/News/Articles/2018/05/23/mcs052318-russian-federation-staff-concluding-statement-of-the-2018-article-iv

———, *People's Republic of China: 2018 Article IV Consultation*, press release; staff report; staff statement and statement by the Executive Director for the People's Republic of China, IMF Country Report No. 18/240, July 2018b. As of December 24, 2018:
https://www.imf.org/en/Publications/CR/Issues/2018/07/25/Peoples-Republic-of-China-2018-Article-IV-Consultation-Press-Release-Staff-Report-Staff-46121

———, Currency Composition of Official Foreign Exchange Reserves (COFER), July 2, 2018c.

"Is It a Risk for America That China Holds over $1 Trillion in U.S. Debt?" China Power, February 2, 2016. As of December 24, 2018:
https://chinapower.csis.org/us-debt

Jackson, Matthew O., and Massimo Morelli, "The Reasons for Wars: An Updated Survey," in Christopher J. Coyne and Rachel L. Mathers, eds., *The Handbook on the Political Economy of War*, Cheltenham, UK, and Northampton, Mass.: Edward Elgar, 2011, Chapter 3, pp. 34–57.

James, Harold, *The End of Globalization: Lessons from the Great Depression*, Cambridge, Mass.: Harvard University Press, 2002.

Janeway, Diane, and Guy Eastman, "US DoD FY19 Budget 'In Depth' Analysis," IHS Jane's, March 15, 2018.

Johnson, Reuben, "Russia to Ramp-Up Production of Sukhoi Su-34," AINonline.com, April 10, 2017.

Johnston, Trevor, Troy D. Smith, and J. Luke Irwin, *Additive Manufacturing in 2040: Powerful Enabler, Disruptive Threat*, Santa Monica, Calif.: RAND Corporation, PE-283-RC, 2018. As of March 4, 2019: https://www.rand.org/pubs/perspectives/PE283.html

Kang, Joong Shik, Sally Chen, and Daniel Law, "Credit Booms—Is China Different?" in International Monetary Fund, *People's Republic of China: Selected Issues*, Washington, D.C., IMF Country Report No. 17/248, August 2017. As of June 28, 2018: http://www.imf.org/en/Publications/CR/Issues/2017/08/15/People-s-Republic-of-China-Selected-Issues-45171

Kaplan, Robert S., "A Perspective on Oil," Federal Reserve Bank of Dallas, June 19, 2018. As of July 1, 2018: https://www.dallasfed.org/news/speeches/kaplan/2018/rsk180619

Kasymov, Shavkat, "Disputes over Water Resources: A History of Conflict and Cooperation in Drainage Basins," *Peace and Conflict Studies*, Vol. 18, No. 2, Article 5, November 1, 2011.

"Kazakhstan to Acquire Additional Su-30SM Fighters from Russia," Defense-Aerospace.com, March 11, 2018.

Keating, Edward G., Irv Blickstein, Michael Boito, Jess Chandler, and Deborah Peetz, *Evaluating the Desirability of Navy F/A-18E/F Service Life Extension Programs (SLEPs)*, Santa Monica, Calif.: RAND Corporation, TR-844-NAVY, 2010. As of March 2, 2019: https://www.rand.org/pubs/technical_reports/TR844.html

"Key Facts About Russia's Su-30 Multirole Fighter Jet," TASS Russian News Agency, May 3, 2018.

Klemmt, Tuke, Rashid Faraby, and Katherine Multop, "Additive Manufacturing: Fundamental Concepts," Washington, D.C., Defense Acquisition University (DAU) briefing, February 7, 2018.

Kynge, James, "China Purchases of Overseas Ports Top $20bn in Past Year," *Financial Times*, July 16, 2017.

Lagarde, Christine, "Belt and Road Initiative: Strategies to Deliver in the Next Phase," Beijing, speech at IMF-PBC Conference, April 12, 2018.

Lardy, Nicholas R., "Issues in China's WTO Accession," Washington, D.C., Brookings Institution, testimony, May 9, 2001. As of June 28, 2018: https://www.brookings.edu/testimonies/issues-in-chinas-wto-accession/

Lee, Jong-Wha, and Ju Hyun Pyun, *Does Trade Integration Contribute to Peace?* Mandaluyong, Philippines: Asian Development Bank, Working Paper Series on Regional Integration No. 24, January 2009.

Leffler, Melvyn P., "From the Truman Doctrine to the Carter Doctrine: Lessons and Dilemmas of the Cold War," *Diplomatic History*, Vol. 7, No. 4, October 1983, pp. 245–266.

Legon, Ronald P., "The Megarian Decree and the Balance of Greek Naval Power," *Classical Philology*, Vol. 68, No. 3, July 1973, pp. 161–171.

Lester, Simon, "Why China's Entry into the WTO Has Been Good for the U.S.," *MarketWatch*, January 23, 2018. As of June 28, 2018:
https://www.marketwatch.com/story/why-chinas-entry-into-the-wto-has-been-good-for-the-us-2018-01-23

Levy, Philip, "Was Letting China into the WTO a Mistake?" *Foreign Affairs*, April 2, 2018. As of June 28, 2018:
https://www.foreignaffairs.com/articles/china/2018-04-02/was-letting-china-wto-mistake

Libicki, Martin C., Howard J. Shatz, and Julie E. Taylor, *Global Demographic Change and Its Implications for Military Power*, Santa Monica, Calif.: RAND Corporation, MG-1091-AF, 2011. As of July 4, 2018:
https://www.rand.org/pubs/monographs/MG1091.html

Litovkin, Victor, "Three Aircraft in One," *Russia Beyond*, March 8, 2012.

Lockheed Martin, "Pentagon and Lockheed Martin Deliver 300th F-35 Aircraft," press release, June 11, 2018.

Lorell, Mark A., Michael Kennedy, Robert S. Leonard, Ken Munson, Shmuel Abramzon, David L. An, and Robert A. Guffey, *Do Joint Fighter Programs Save Money?* Santa Monica, Calif.: RAND Corporation, MG-1225-AF, 2013. As of March 4, 2019:
https://www.rand.org/pubs/monographs/MG1225.html

Lorell, Mark, Julia Lowell, Richard M. Moore, Victoria Greenfield, and Katia Vlachos-Dengler, *Going Global? U.S. Government Policy and the Defense Aerospace Industry*, Santa Monica, Calif.: RAND Corporation, MR-1537-AF, 2002. As of March 2, 2019:
https://www.rand.org/pubs/monograph_reports/MR1537.html

MacDougall, James C., "Review Essay: Destined for War: Can America and China Escape Thucydides's Trap?" *Parameters*, Vol. 47, No. 2, Summer 2017, pp. 113–116.

"'Made in China 2025' Plan Unveiled," Xinhua, May 19, 2015. As of December 17, 2018:
http://www.xinhuanet.com/english/2015-05/19/c_134251770.htm

Majumdar, Dave, "The JAS-39 Gripen: Sweden's Cheap (and Deadly) Fighter Plane," *The National Interest*, September 24, 2015.

Mansfield, Edward D., *Power, Trade, and War*, Princeton, N.J.: Princeton University Press, 1994.

Markusen, Ann, "The Economics of Defence Industry Mergers and Divestitures," *Economic Affairs*, Vol. 17, No. 4, December 1997, pp. 28–32.

Martin, Bradley, Michael E. McMahon, Jessie Riposo, James G. Kallimani, Angelena Bohman, Alyssa Ramos, and Abby Schendt, *A Strategic Assessment of the Future of U.S. Navy Ship Maintenance: Challenges and Opportunities*, Santa Monica, Calif.: RAND Corporation, RR-1951-NAVY, 2017. As of March 4, 2019: https://www.rand.org/pubs/research_reports/RR1951.html

Martin, Philippe, Thierry Mayer, and Mathias Thoenig, "Make Trade Not War?" *Review of Economic Studies*, Vol. 75, 2008, pp. 865–900.

Maugeri, Leonardo, *The Age of Oil: The Mythology, History, and Future of the World's Most Controversial Resource*, Westport, Conn., and London: Praeger, 2006.

Mazarr, Michael J., Timothy R. Heath, and Astrid Stuth Cevallos, *China and the International Order*, Santa Monica, Calif.: RAND Corporation, RR-2423-OSD, 2018. As of July 15, 2018:
https://www.rand.org/pubs/research_reports/RR2423.html

McCrae, Michael Allan, "China Denies Withholding Rare Earth Metals from Japan," Mining.com, September 23, 2010. As of June 30, 2018:
http://www.mining.com/china-denies-withholding-rare-earth-metals-from-japan/

McDowell, Daniel, and David A. Steinberg, "Systemic Strengths, Domestic Deficiencies: The Renminbi's Future as a Reserve Currency," *Journal of Contemporary China*, Vol. 26, No. 108, 2017, pp. 801–819.

McGregor, Tom, "China Breakthroughs: New International Payments System Goes into Action," CCTV.com, October 19, 2017. As of July 4, 2018:
http://english.cctv.com/2017/10/19/ARTIXz5AbEqSewRu8jDIFRKO171019.shtml

McGuire, Martin C., "Economics of Defense in a Globalized World," in Todd Sandler and Keith Hartley, eds., *Handbook of Defense Economics*, Vol. 2, Amsterdam: Elsevier B.V., 2007, Ch. 21, pp. 623–648.

McLeary, Paul, "Defense Industry Running Out of Time; Mergers Loom," *Defense News*, January 9, 2015.

Meese, Michael J., Suzanne C. Nielsen, and Rachel M. Sondheimer, *American National Security*, 7th ed., Baltimore, Md.: Johns Hopkins University Press, 2018.

Mehta, Aaron, "The US Is Running Out of Bombs—and It May Soon Struggle to Make More," *Defense News*, May 22, 2018.

Mintz, John, "How a Dinner Led to a Feeding Frenzy," *Washington Post*, July 4, 1997.

"More Russian Su-35 Fighters Rumored to Join PLAAF," *Asia Times*, March 9, 2018.

Morelli, Massimo, and Tommaso Sonno, "On Economic Interdependence and War," *Journal of Economic Literature*, Vol. 55, No. 3, 2017, pp. 1084–1097.

Morgan, Forrest E., and Raphael S. Cohen, *Military Trends and the Future of Warfare: The Changing Global Environment and Its Implications for the U.S. Air Force*, RR-2849/3-AF, Santa Monica, Calif.: RAND Corporation, 2020. As of May 2020:
https://www.rand.org/pubs/research_reports/RR2849z3.html

Mouchantaf, Chirine, "Lockheed Keeps F-16 Production Line Going with Bahrain Deal," *Defense News*, January 19, 2018.

National Development and Reform Commission, *Vision and Actions on Jointly Building Silk Road Economic Belt and 21st-Century Maritime Silk Road*, Beijing: Ministry of Foreign Affairs, Ministry of Commerce of the People's Republic of China, with State Council Authorization, March 28, 2015.

National Foundation for American Policy, "The Importance of International Students to American Science and Engineering," Arlington, Va., NFAP Policy Brief, October 2017.

NATO—*See* North Atlantic Treaty Organization.

Naughton, Barry, "Economic Policy in the Aftermath of the 19th Party Congress," *China Leadership Monitor*, No. 55, January 23, 2018. As of December 24, 2018:
https://www.hoover.org/research/economic-policy-aftermath-19th-party-congress

Negishi, Mayumi, "Japan Hopes Rare-Earth Find Will Give It an Edge Against China," *Wall Street Journal*, April 11, 2018. As of July 1, 2018:
https://www.wsj.com/articles/japan-hopes-rare-earth-find-will-give-it-an-edge-against-china-1523446948

North Atlantic Treaty Organization, "Defence Expenditures of NATO Countries (2010–2017)," Brussels, press release, Communique PR/CP (2018) 16, March 15, 2018a. As of July 5, 2018:
https://www.nato.int/cps/ie/natohq/news_152830.htm

———, "Member Countries," webpage, March 26, 2018b. As of December 18, 2018:
https://www.nato.int/cps/em/natohq/topics_52044.htm

Office of the Secretary of Defense, *Fiscal Year 2016 Annual Industrial Capabilities Report to Congress*, Washington, D.C., April 2017.

———, *Fiscal Year 2017 Annual Industrial Capabilities Report to Congress*, Washington, D.C., March 2018.

Oneal, John R., Frances H. Oneal, Zeev Maoz, and Bruce Russett, "The Liberal Peace: Interdependence, Democracy, and International Conflict, 1950–1985," *Journal of Peace Research*, Vol. 33, No. 1, February 1996, pp. 11–28.

Organisation for Economic Co-operation and Development, *OECD Economic Surveys 1981–1982: Germany*, Paris, June 1982.

———, *OECD Economic Surveys: Germany 1990/1991*, Paris, 1991.

———, *Education at a Glance 2011*, Paris, 2011.

O'Rourke, Ronald, *Navy Force Structure and Shipbuilding Plans: Background and Issues for Congress*, Washington, D.C.: Congressional Research Service, RL32665, July 31, 2018.

Osborne, Tony, "Typhoon Production Nudges to 2023," *ShowNews*, June 18, 2017.

Padhi, Catherine, "Emergencies Without End: A Primer on Federal States of Emergency," *Lawfare*, December 8, 2017. As of July 3, 2018:
https://www.lawfareblog.com/
emergencies-without-end-primer-federal-states-emergency

Pak, Jin H., "China, India, and War over Water," *Parameters*, Vol. 46, No. 2, Summer 2016, pp. 53–67.

Patterson, Scott, and Russell Gold, "There's a Global Race to Control Batteries—and China Is Winning," *Wall Street Journal*, February 11, 2018.

Paxton, Matthew O., "Testimony of Matthew O. Paxton, President, Shipbuilders Council of America, before the United States Senate Committee on Armed Services, Subcommittee on Seapower, [on] Industry Perspectives on Options and Considerations for Achieving a 355-Ship Navy," Washington, D.C., May 24, 2017.

Pei, Minxin, "US-China Conflict Risks New Cold War," *Nikkei Asian Review*, January 24, 2018. As of July 24, 2018:
https://asia.nikkei.com/Politics/US-China-conflict-risks-new-Cold-War

Pettis, Michael, "China's Growth Miracle Has Run Out of Steam," *Financial Times*, November 19, 2017. As of June 28, 2018:
https://www.ft.com/content/cb6bbf84-cb8e-11e7-ab18-7a9fb7d6163e

———, "China Was Never Likely to Have a Debt Crisis," CNBC, February 28, 2018. As of July 24, 2018:
https://carnegieendowment.org/2018/02/28/
china-was-never-likely-to-have-debt-crisis-pub-75719

Polachek, Solomon, Carlos Seiglie, and Jun Xiang, "The Impact of Foreign Direct Investment on International Conflict," *Defence and Peace Economics*, Vol. 18, No. 5, 2007, pp. 415–429.

Polk, Andrew, "China Is Quietly Setting Global Standards," Bloomberg, May 6, 2018.

Pons, Corina, "Exclusive: Venezuela Faces Heavy Bill as Grace Period Lapses on China Loans—Source," Reuters, April 27, 2018. As of July 24, 2018:
https://www.reuters.com/article/us-venezuela-china/exclusive-venezuela-faces-heavy-bill-as-grace-period-lapses-on-china-loans-sources-idUSKBN1HY2K0

Potholm, Christian P., *Winning at War: Seven Keys to Military Victory Throughout History*, Lanham, Md.: Rowman & Littlefield, 2010.

Public Law 115-44, Countering America's Adversaries Through Sanctions Act, August 2, 2017.

"Revision of Democratic Republic of Congo's Mining Code Driven by Cobalt Price Rise," Dentons, July 2, 2018. As of July 24, 2018:
https://www.dentons.com/en/insights/alerts/2018/july/2/revision-of-democratic-republic-of-congos-mining-code-driven-by-cobalt-price-rise

Robbins, Lionel, *The Economic Causes of War*, New York: Howard Fertig, 1968.

"Russia May Start Exporting Advanced MiG-35 Fighter Jet in Couple of Years," TASS Russian News Agency, June 19, 2017.

"Russia to Reschedule Su-30SM Fighter Delivery to Belarus over Technical Changes," DefenseWorld.net, July 18, 2017.

Russian Direct Investment Fund, "Russian Direct Investment Fund and Vietnamese State Capital Investment Corporation to Create a $500 Million Russian-Vietnamese Investment Platform," press release, May 16, 2016a.

———, "NIIF and RDIF to Establish a $1BN Russian Indian Investment Fund," press release, October 15, 2016b.

———, "RCIF and Tus-Holdings to Create Russia-China Venture Fund," press release, November 7, 2016c.

———, "RDIF and JBIC Agree Key Terms and Conditions for Russia-Japan Investment Fund," press release, April 27, 2017.

Salidjanova, Nargiza, "China's Stock Market Collapse and Government's Response," Issue Brief, U.S.-China Economic and Security Review Commission, July 13, 2015. As of July 19, 2018:
https://www.uscc.gov/sites/default/files/Research/China%E2%80%99s%20Stock%20Market%20Collapse%20and%20Government%E2%80%99s%20Response.pdf

Sanderson, Henry, "China Tightens Grip on Global Cobalt Supplies," *Financial Times*, March 14, 2018a. As of August 27, 2018:
https://www.ft.com/content/86dc1306-27a4-11e8-b27e-cc62a39d57a0

———, "Electric Cars: The Race to Replace Cobalt," *Financial Times*, August 20, 2018b. As of August 27, 2018:
https://www.ft.com/content/3b72645a-91cc-11e8-bb8f-a6a2f7bca546

Schneider, Greg, and Renae Merle, "Reagan's Defense Buildup Bridged Military Eras," *Washington Post*, June 9, 2004.

Schulz, Klaus J., Nadine M. Piatak, and John F. Papp, "Niobium and Tantalum," in Klaus J. Schulz, John H. DeYoung, Jr., Robert R. Seal II, and Dwight C. Bradley, eds., *Critical Mineral Resources of the United States—Economic and Environmental Geology and Prospects for Future Supply*, Washington, D.C.: U.S. Geological Survey, U.S. Department of the Interior, Professional Paper 1802–M, 2017, Chapter M.

Scobell, Andrew, Bonny Lin, Howard J. Shatz, Michael Johnson, Larry Hanauer, Michael S. Chase, Astrid Stuth Cevallos, Ivan W. Rasmussen, Arthur Chan, Aaron Strong, Eric Warner, and Logan Ma, *At the Dawn of Belt and Road: China in the Developing World*, Santa Monica, Calif.: RAND Corporation, RR-2273-A, 2018. As of March 2, 2019:
https://www.rand.org/pubs/research_reports/RR2273.html

Setser, Brad W., "What Would Happen If China Started Selling Off Its Treasury Portfolio?" Washington, D.C., Council on Foreign Relations, June 21, 2018. As of December 24, 2018:
https://www.cfr.org/blog/what-would-happen-if-china-started-selling-its-treasury-portfolio

Shalal, Andrea, "U.S. Arms Makers Strain to Meet Demand as Mideast Conflicts Rage," Reuters, December 4, 2015.

Shatz, Howard, "The Long-Term Budget Shortfall and National Security: A Problem the United States Should Stop Avoiding," *War on the Rocks*, November 6, 2017. As of July 25, 2018:
https://warontherocks.com/2017/11/the-long-term-budget-shortfall-and-national-security-a-problem-the-united-states-should-stop-avoiding/

Shatz, Howard J., and David A. Shlapak, "The Made-in-America Global Security and Economic System Still Serves U.S. Interests," *Plain Dealer*, October 19, 2016. As of July 6, 2018:
https://www.cleveland.com/opinion/index.ssf/2016/10/the_made-in-america_global_sec.html

Shinkman, Paul, "ISIS War Drains U.S. Bomb Supply," *U.S. News and World Report*, February 17, 2017.

Shukla, Ajai, "Lockheed Martin Says F-16 Orders Flowing In," *Business Standard*, December 16, 2017.

Silberglitt, Richard, James T. Bartis, Brian G. Chow, David L. An, and Kyle Brady, *Critical Materials: Present Danger to U.S. Manufacturing*, Santa Monica, Calif.: RAND Corporation, RR-133-NIC, 2013. As of July 1, 2018:
https://www.rand.org/pubs/research_reports/RR133.html

Stevenson, Beth, "Gripen Production Line Established in Brazil," IHS Jane's Defence Industry, May 10, 2018.

Stockholm International Peace Research Institute, "SIPRI Military Expenditure Database," Solna, Sweden, undated. As of July 4, 2018:
https://www.sipri.org/databases/milex

———, *SIPRI Arms Industry Database 2017*, Solna, Sweden, 2017.

Sullivan, Declan, "Destined for Competition: An Analysis of Graham Allison's Thucydides Trap," *The Strategy Bridge*, January 24, 2018. As of August 29, 2018:
https://thestrategybridge.org/the-bridge/2018/1/24/destined-for-competition-an-analysis-of-graham-allisons-thucydides-trap

Taleb, Nassim Nicholas, *The Black Swan: The Impact of the Highly Improbable*, New York: Random House, 2007.

———, *Antifragile: Things That Gain from Disorder*, New York: Random House, 2012.

Takaya, Yutaro, Kazutaka Yasukawa, Takehiro Kawasaki, Koichiro Fujinaga, Junichiro Ohta, Yoichi Usui, Kentaro Nakamura, Jun-Ichi Kimura, Qing Chang, Morihisa Hamada, Gjergj Dodbiba, Tatsuo Nozaki, Koichi Iijima, Tomohiro Morisawa, Takuma Kuwahara, Yasuyuki Ishida, Takao Ichimura, Masaki Kitazume, Toyohisa Fujita, and Yasuhiro Kato, "The Tremendous Potential of Deep-Sea Mud as a Source of Rare-Earth Elements," *Nature*, April 10, 2018. As of July 1, 2018:
https://www.nature.com/articles/s41598-018-23948-5.pdf

Thompson, Mark, "The Defense Dinosaurs," *Time*, September 29, 2011.

Thorne, Devin, and Ben Spevack, *Harbored Ambitions: How China's Port Investments Are Strategically Reshaping the Indo-Pacific*, Washington, D.C., C4ADS, April 2018.

Tirpak, John, "Munitions Production Surge Planned for At Least Five Years," *Air Force Magazine*, February 22, 2018.

Torbat, Akbar E., "Impacts of the US Trade and Financial Sanctions on Iran," *The World Economy*, Vol. 28, No. 3, 2005, pp. 407–434.

Tran, Pierre, "Dassault Credits Rafale Export Deals as Financial Savior," *Defense News*, March 8, 2017.

Truman, Edwin M., "The Chinese Renminbi Is Not a Freely Usable Currency Yet," Washington, D.C.: Peterson Institute for International Economics, August 7, 2015. As of June 26, 2018:
https://piie.com/blogs/realtime-economic-issues-watch/chinese-renminbi-not-freely-usable-currency-yet

United Aircraft Corporation, "About UAC: History," webpage, undated. As of July 6, 2018:
https://www.uacrussia.ru/en/corporation/history/

United Nations, "National Accounts Main Aggregates Database," online database, December 2017. As of March 11, 2018:
https://unstats.un.org/unsd/snaama/

United Nations Conference on Trade and Development, "Foreign Direct Investment: Inward and Outward Flows and Stock, Annual, 1970–2016," database, undated. As of March 11, 2019:
https://unctadstat.unctad.org/wds/ReportFolders/reportFolders.aspx

United Nations Conference on Trade and Development Secretariat, *Services, Development and Trade: The Regulatory and Institutional Dimension*, Geneva, Switzerland, TD/B/C.I/MEM.4/11, March 9, 2016. As of December 24, 2018:
https://unctad.org/meetings/en/SessionalDocuments/c1mem4d11_en.pdf

U.S. Chamber of Commerce, *Made in China 2025: Global Ambitions Built on Local Protections*, Washington, D.C., 2017.

U.S. Congressional Budget Office, *Costs of Building a 355-Ship Navy*, Washington, D.C., April 2017.

———, *The Budget and Economic Outlook: 2018 to 2028*, Washington, D.C., April 2018a. As of December 19, 2018:
https://www.cbo.gov/publication/53651

———, *The 2018 Long-Term Budget Outlook*, Washington, D.C., June 2018b. As of July 24, 2018:
https://www.cbo.gov/publication/53919

U.S. Department of Commerce, Office of Public Affairs, "U.S. Department of Commerce Initiates Section 232 Investigation into Uranium Imports," Washington, D.C., press release, July 18, 2018. As of July 24, 2018:
https://www.commerce.gov/news/press-releases/2018/07/us-department-commerce-initiates-section-232-investigation-uranium

U.S. Department of Defense, *Strategic and Critical Materials Operations Report to Congress: Operations Under the Strategic and Critical Materials Stock Piling Act During Fiscal Year 2016*, Washington, D.C.: Defense Logistics Agency Strategic Materials, Office of the Under Secretary of Defense for Acquisition, Technology, and Logistics, January 2017. As of May 28, 2019:
https://www.dla.mil/Portals/104/Documents/StrategicMaterials/Reports/Operations%20Report/FY16%20Operations%20Report_FINAL_Website%20Version.pdf?ver=2017-03-29-080514-340

———, *Summary of the 2018 National Defense Strategy of the United States of America: Sharpening the American Military's Competitive Edge*, Washington, D.C., 2018a.

———, *Assessing and Strengthening the Manufacturing and Defense Industrial Base and Supply Chain Resiliency of the United States*, report to President Donald J. Trump by the Interagency Task Force in Fulfillment of Executive Order 13806, September 2018b.

U.S. Department of Energy, Office of Fossil Energy, "Strategic Petroleum Reserve," webpage, undated. As of December 20, 2018:
https://www.energy.gov/fe/services/petroleum-reserves/strategic-petroleum-reserve

U.S. Department of the Interior, "Final List of Critical Minerals 2018," *Federal Register*, Vol. 83, No. 97, May 18, 2018, pp. 23295–23296.

U.S. Department of the Interior, Office of the Secretary, "Draft List of Critical Minerals," *Federal Register*, Vol. 83, No. 33, February 16, 2018, pp. 7065–7068. As of July 1, 2018:
https://www.federalregister.gov/documents/2018/02/16/2018-03219/draft-list-of-critical-minerals

U.S. Department of State, Office of the Historian, Bureau of Public Affairs, "The Warsaw Treaty Organization, 1955," webpage, undated. As of December 18, 2018:
https://history.state.gov/milestones/1953-1960/warsaw-treaty

U.S. Department of State, U.S. Department of Defense, U.S. Department of Interior, and U.S. Department of Justice, *Report to the National Security Council by the Departments of State, Defense, the Interior, and Justice*, Washington, D.C., NSC 138/1, January 6, 1953 (via Office of the Historian, U.S. Department of State). As of July 1, 2018:
https://history.state.gov/historicaldocuments/frus1952-54v01p2/d159

U.S. Department of the Treasury, "Treasury Designates Banco Delta Asia as Primary Money Laundering Concern Under USA PATRIOT Act," Washington, D.C., Press Release JS-2720, September 15, 2005. As of July 3, 2018:
https://www.treasury.gov/press-center/press-releases/Pages/js2720.aspx

———, "Fact Sheet: New Sanctions on Iran," Washington, D.C., November 21, 2011. As of July 3, 2018:
https://www.treasury.gov/press-center/press-releases/Pages/tg1367.aspx

———, *Monthly Treasury Statement: Receipts and Outlays of the United States Government for Fiscal Year 2019 Through October 31, 2018, and Other Periods*, Washington, D.C.: Bureau of the Fiscal Service, 2018. As of December 24, 2018:
https://www.fiscal.treasury.gov/files/reports-statements/mts/mts1018.pdf

———, "Major Foreign Holders of Treasury Securities," online data, December 17, 2018. As of December 24, 2018:
http://ticdata.treasury.gov/Publish/mfh.txt

U.S. Geological Survey, "Rare Earths: Statistics and Information," webpage, March 30, 2018. As of August 27, 2018:
https://minerals.usgs.gov/minerals/pubs/commodity/rare_earths/

U.S. Trade Representative, "United States Wins Victory in Rare Earths Dispute with China: WTO Report Finds China's Export Restraints Breach WTO Rules," press release, March 26, 2014. As of June 30, 2018:
https://ustr.gov/about-us/policy-offices/press-office/press-releases/2014/March/US-wins-victory-in-rare-earths-dispute-with-China

———, *2017 Report to Congress on China's WTO Compliance*, Washington, D.C., January 2018a.

———, "USTR Issues Tariffs on Chinese Products in Response to Unfair Trade Practices," Press Release, Washington, D.C., June 15, 2018b. As of June 29, 2018: https://ustr.gov/about-us/policy-offices/press-office/press-releases/2018/june/ustr-issues-tariffs-chinese-products

van der Kamp, Jake, "My Prediction: The Coming Collapse of China's Ponzi Scheme Economy," *South China Morning Post*, August 27, 2017. As of July 24, 2018:
https://www.scmp.com/print/news/article/2108442/my-prediction-coming-collapse-chinas-ponzi-scheme-economy

VanGrasstek, Craig, *The History and Future of the World Trade Organization*, Geneva: World Trade Organization, 2013.

Vasta, Sameer, "World Bank Gets Capital Increase and Reforms Voting Power," *Voices*, World Bank Blog, April 25, 2010.

Véron, Nicolas, "EU Financial Services Policy Since 2007: Crisis, Responses and Prospects," *Global Policy*, Vol. 9, Supplement 1, June 2018, pp. 54–64.

Victor, David G., "What Resource Wars?" *The National Interest*, November 12, 2007. As of July 24, 2018:
https://nationalinterest.org/article/what-resource-wars-1851

Vogt, Bill, "What You Can Do When You Have To," *Target*, Vol. 15, No. 1, First Quarter, 1999.

von Mises, Ludwig, "The Economic Causes of War," lecture delivered in Orange County, California, in October 1944, reprinted in *The Freeman*, April 2004.

Wayne, Leslie, "Lockheed Cancels Northrop Merger, Citing U.S. Stand," *New York Times*, July 17, 1998.

Weisgerber, Marcus, "Pentagon Worried About Defense Contractor Monopolies," *Fiscal Times*, October 3, 2015.

———, "America's Last Fighter Jet Makers Scramble to Keep Production Alive," *DefenseOne*, May 12, 2016.

White House, *State of the Union Address Delivered Before a Joint Session of the Congress*, January 23, 1980. As of July 1, 2018:
http://www.presidency.ucsb.edu/ws/index.php?pid=33079

———, *Assessing and Strengthening the Manufacturing and Defense Industrial Base and Supply Chain Resiliency of the United States*, Washington, D.C.: Executive Order 13806, July 21, 2017a.

———, *National Security Strategy of the United States*, Washington, D.C., December 2017b. As of June 28, 2018:
https://www.whitehouse.gov/wp-content/uploads/2017/12/NSS-Final-12-18-2017-0905.pdf

———, *A Federal Strategy to Ensure Secure and Reliable Supplies of Critical Minerals*, Washington, D.C.: Executive Order 13817, December 20, 2017c, via *Federal Register*, Vol. 82, No. 246, December 26, 2017, pp. 60835–60837. As of July 25, 2018:
https://www.gpo.gov/fdsys/granule/FR-2017-12-26/2017-27899

Williams, Lynn M., and Heidi M. Peters, "Defense Primer: Future Years Defense Program (FYDP)," Washington, D.C., Congressional Research Service, IF 10831, February 16, 2018. As of December 14, 2018:
https://fas.org/sgp/crs/natsec/IF10831.pdf

World Bank, *World Development Report 2011: Conflict, Security, and Development*, Washington, D.C., 2011.

———, *World Development Indicators*, November 14, 2018. As of March 2, 2019:
http://datatopics.worldbank.org/world-development-indicators/

World Trade Organization, "China," webpage, undated-a. As of June 28, 2018:
https://www.wto.org/english/thewto_e/acc_e/a1_chine_e.htm

———, "The Doha Round," webpage, undated-b. As of December 17, 2018:
https://www.wto.org/english/tratop_e/dda_e/dda_e.htm

———, "The GATT Years: From Havana to Marrakech," webpage, undated-c. As of December 17, 2018:
https://www.wto.org/english/thewto_e/whatis_e/tif_e/fact4_e.htm#rounds

———, "Members and Observers," webpage, undated-d. As of June 26, 2018:
https://www.wto.org/english/thewto_e/whatis_e/tif_e/org6_e.htm

———, "Statistics on Merchandise Trade," online database, undated-e. As of June 26, 2018:
https://www.wto.org/english/res_e/statis_e/merch_trade_stat_e.htm

———, "What We Do," webpage, undated-f. As of June 26, 2018:
https://www.wto.org/english/thewto_e/whatis_e/what_we_do_e.htm

———, *WTO Statistics Data Sets–Metadata*, undated-g. As of December 17, 2018:
http://stat.wto.org/StatisticalProgram/WSDBStatProgramTechNotes.aspx?Language=E#Def_Meth_Ind

———, *World Trade Report 2013: Factors Shaping the Future of World Trade*, Geneva, 2013.

———, "Trade and Tariffs: Trade Grows as Tariffs Decline," Geneva, brochure, 2015a.

———, "DS431: China—Measures Related to the Exportation of Rare Earths, Tungsten and Molybdenum," webpage, May 20, 2015b. As of June 30, 2018: https://www.wto.org/english/tratop_e/dispu_e/cases_e/ds431_e.htm

Wright, Thomas, "A Special Argument: The U.S., the U.K., and the AIIB," Brookings Institution, March 13, 2015. As of December 17, 2018: https://www.brookings.edu/blog/order-from-chaos/2015/03/13/a-special-argument-the-u-s-u-k-and-the-aiib/

WTO—*See* World Trade Organization.

Wübbeke, Jost, Mirjam Meissner, Max J. Zenglein, Jaqueline Ives, and Björn Conrad, *Made in China 2025: The Making of a High-Tech Superpower and Consequences for Industrial Countries*, Berlin: Mercator Institute for China Studies, MERICS Papers on China No. 2, December 2016. As of December 17, 2018: https://www.merics.org/en/papers-on-china/made-china-2025

Xi Jinping, "Secure a Decisive Victory in Building a Moderately Prosperous Society in All Respects and Strive for the Great Success of Socialism with Chinese Characteristics for a New Era," full text of Xi Jinping's report at the 19th CPC National Congress, delivered at the 19th National Congress of the Communist Party of China, October 18, 2017. As of June 29, 2018: http://www.chinadaily.com.cn/china/19thcpcnationalcongress/2017-11/04/content_34115212.htm

Yang, Jiawen, Hossein Askari, John Forrer, and Hildy Teegen, "U.S. Economic Sanctions: An Empirical Study," *International Trade Journal*, Vol. 18, No. 1, Spring 2004, pp. 23–62.

Younossi, Obaid, Kevin Brancato, John C. Graser, Thomas Light, Rena Rudavsky, and Jerry Sollinger, *Ending F-22A Production: Costs and Industrial Base Implications of Alternative Options*, Santa Monica, Calif.: RAND Corporation, MG-797-AF, 2010. As of March 2, 2019: https://www.rand.org/pubs/monographs/MG797.html

Zarate, Juan C., *Treasury's War: The Unleashing of a New Era of Financial Warfare*, New York: Public Affairs, 2013.

Zhang Zhengfu, Liu Jie, and Wang Xiuqiong, "China Focus: How China Can Avoid the Middle Income Trap in a New Era," *Xinhua*, October 23, 2017. As of July 19, 2018: http://www.xinhuanet.com/english/2017-10/23/c_136699982.htm

Zumbrun, Josh, "How China and the U.S. Both Come Out Winners in Boost to World Bank," *Wall Street Journal*, April 23, 2018. As of June 28, 2018: https://blogs.wsj.com/economics/2018/04/23/how-china-and-the-u-s-both-come-out-winners-in-the-world-banks-funding-increase/

Printed in the USA
CPSIA information can be obtained
at www.ICGtesting.com
LVHW062037260824
789300LV00002B/321

9 781977 402981